A GUIDE TO
THE FILM INDUSTRY
Philip Rand

Emerald Publishing

Emerald Publishing
61 Inniskilling Road
London E13 9LD

© Emerald Publishing 2003

British Library Cataloguing in publication data. A Catalogue record for this book is available from the British Library.

ISBN 1903190912 0

Cover design by Bookworks Ltd

Printed by Bookcraft, Wiltshire.

A Guide to the Film Industry

CONTENTS

Introduction

vii

INTRODUCTION

The film industry is, without doubt, very complex and costly, employing legions of people working within what often resembles a military operation. In turn, the goal of this operation (the making of a feature film) is to ensure that the general public flock to the cinema, often completely brainwashed by 'hype' to witness the thrill of this film and hopefully return a profit to the makers.

What the general public usually do not comprehend is the massive complexity involved in making a feature film, the roles of the many people involved, the sources of finance and the all-important roles of the producer and director. The average cinema-goer witnesses the end product of many months, sometimes years, work and, in many cases, the expenditure of many millions of dollars or pounds on the marketing of the film (the hype).

For a successful film the rewards are enormous, for both the producers and the stars. For the failures, and there are many, this can break the company and have a negative impact on the stars. What then, is the film business? What is the history of the film industry in this country and the rest of the world, especially the USA? What is the current approach to the film industry, particularly on the part of the government which has played an important historical role?

This book looks initially at these questions and then outlines the business of film, the financing, and looks at the roles of the players in the process, following with a look at the making of a feature film. It also looks at the growing animation industry along with commercials and documentaries.

Finally, the book outlines a range of organisations and courses on offer to the person interested in entering the film industry and developing a career. Very much a practical book, A Guide to The Film Industry is a must for anyone interested in the industry, whether as an interested observer or a s a would-be filmmaker.

-1-
The Film Business - Looking Back

The origins of filmmaking

To see just how far the film business has developed during the last century we have to travel back to the very first films. The first motion pictures were very basic affairs indeed, two-dimensional, black and white and extremely short, often of one or two-minute duration. These films were shown on a 'kinetoscope', developed by Thomas Edison in 1889. The first public kinetoscope parlour was opened by Edison in 1894, in New York.

Like many such developments in technology at that time, the basic principles of cinema had in fact been known for centuries, going as far back as the sixteenth century in Italy. Like a lot of major developments, however, the nineteenth century saw the first real breakthrough in motion pictures.

In Britain, the Lumiere brother's films were shown on a Cinematographe at the Marlborough Hall in Regent Street, London in 1896. This event is seen as the birth of commercial cinema in this country. A small admission charge was made and the films, under one minute each, included 'workers leaving the Lumiere factory', 'Watering the Gardener' and 'Congress of Photographic Studies'.

Following an enthusiastic response the Cinematographe was moved to the Empire Music Hall in Leicester Square for a series of nightly performances that continued for 18 months. (It is not sure whether popcorn was sold at this stage or not. The popcorn revolution had yet to begin).

These then, were the early beginnings of commercial cinema and, at the time, no one involved in the development of the industry could possibly see the vast potential and the ultimate growth of the film business.

The development of picture houses

The music hall was the first real home of the cinema, and short films became an established part of the programme in halls throughout the country. In addition, films began showing in other venues, not cinemas as such, but more specialised venues like the Lewisham Art Club in 1896.

In 1904, Lt Colonel A.C Bromhead, who later became chairman of the Gaumont-British Corporation in the 1920's, opened the daily bioscope in Bishopsgate London. The actual site of this venue was a converted shop holding about 100 people. Two years later, an American called George Hale opened a 'cinema' in Oxford Street in London. These particular premises were also converted from a shop and the conversion took the form of a railway carriage. The audience sat in the carriage and watched travel films through the windows.

Although Hales cinema, which expanded throughout England, was short-lived, the idea took hold and between 1908 and 1945, a transformation took place and cinemas mushroomed.

The pre-war period saw the creation of chains of cinemas, as opposed to single ownership which had been the trend up until then.. Three such chains were Electric Theatres (1908) Biograph Theatres (1908) and Provincial Cinematograph Theatres (1909).

Out of the three chains, the latter group fared particularly well and was to play a very important role in the development of the Gaumont-British Corporation in the late 1920's. By 1913, Provincial Cinematograph Theatres had over 18 cinemas throughout England and also expanded to form the production company, London Film Company. Before the First World War, PCT formed Associated Provincial Picture Theatres Limited.

By the outbreak of the First World War in 1914, there were 109 circuits in Great Britain and, as the number of cinemas grew, the owners realised the need for a representative organisation and the *Cinematograph Exhibitors Association* was formed (constituted in 1912).

Government intervention and regulation of cinema
The rapid growth of cinemas after 1908 became a cause for concern and led to the government intervening on the grounds of public safety. Similar to situations within other industries, the fact that there were so many people grouped together in a public place watching films, alerted the government and other authorities to the potential problems that could occur. *The Cinematograph Films Act*, which became law in 1910, known as the 'showman's charter' allowed local authorities to intervene in the running of cinemas on the basis of 'public well-being'. This meant censorship and Sunday closing, a move which was resisted by the various organisations and business involved. Eventually, a compromise was reached between the government and cinema operators, in the following year, and it was agreed that cinemas could open on a Sunday but all profits would be given to charity. The question of censorship was resolved by the creation of the *British* Board *of Film Censors* with the examiners being independent of the trade. The board began operating in 1913.

Film Distribution in the early years
As cinema chains developed rapidly, so did the film distribution business. Initially, films were purchased directly from producers who published lists of their titles. Both home and export markets flourished. In addition to direct sales, the film rental trade developed rapidly. Rental companies bought their films from producers with the situation arising that films were available for hire or purchase simultaneously.

13

One problem facing the film industry was the determination of the price of a film. Opinion on this matter shifted in the direction of 'exclusivity': one dealer would handle a particular film and have the exclusive rights to its promotion and exhibition. The money paid for exclusives was very significant indeed. Films such as *Quo Vadis* sold for £6700 and reflected the public's taste for quality pictures rather than short films.

The public's continuing demand for feature films of some length, as opposed to short films, was nurtured by American and French Productions. In 1919, France provided 36% of the films released in the UK and the US 28%. Britain came fourth (15%) after Italy (17%).

The move towards feature film inevitably involved higher production costs and financial backing was not so available. The problem was that the British film market was not big enough to justify this kind of investment. The American Market was (and is) big enough and so began American growth in the British film industry. Very early on the Americans allied production and distribution, in the process forming a coherent and effective industry.

Film Production in the early years

Many thousands of films were produced in Britain following the Lumiere Brothers initial showing. They were usually very short, less than a minute's duration. However, as we have seen longer films did make an appearance, with the success of Cecil Hepworths *Falsely Accused* (1906) running for 14 minutes, being a good example of this emerging demand. The most famous film of this period was *Rescued by Rover* (1905) another Hepworth production. This lasted seven minutes. There were about twelve film production companies operating in this period, the most important being those run by Robert W. Paul and Cecil Hepworth. The French Company Gaumont opened an office in London in 1898 and sold imported films and equipment, starting to produce and distribute shortly thereafter, becoming one of the most important selling agents in the world for both British and foreign film.

Early days in America

The film industry in America had very similar beginnings to the British industry. However, due to a totally different approach to business, it rapidly took on a different form. In 1908 the ten major US producers and manufacturers combined to form the Motion Picture Patents Company. This became an effective monopoly with the General Film Company formed in 1910 to control the distribution of all films in the United States.

Not unnaturally, some took exception to these monopolistic developments, one person being William Fox, who continued working as an exhibitor, producer and distributor in his own right. Another who opposed the monopoly was Carl Laemmle the founder of Universal Pictures and the man credited with the growth of the 'star system' in Hollywood. Litigation ensued between the Picture Patents Company and the independents and in 1915 the Federal Court ordered the patents company to be wound up, thereby paving the way for independents.

Right from the outset, the Americans approached the production and marketing of films as a business, their methods far more organised and investment driven than their British counterparts. American domination of the film industry was established right at the outset and has continued to this day.

The growth of the industry through and after the First World War

The Americans gained further dominance throughout the First World War, as a direct result of closures of studios in France Germany and Italy. US film exports almost doubled during this period. There was a brief fall in production and distribution after the Americans entered the war in 1917, but the situation recovered after the end of the war.

The tide of American films began to concern the British government and action took the form of an import tax. British production began to grow but out of 420 films offered for sale in America only six were taken up. While continuing to provide popular films for British audiences in the post-war years, the American industry began to dominate via the distribution side of the business. Given the size of their own market, costs were lower and therefore films could be offered at a cheaper rate in overseas markets. The plight of the British film industry once again became a matter of serious concern by the mid 1920's. British producers were unable to compete with Hollywood, and the American distribution network in London had a stranglehold on the domestic market.

Following representation to the government, several proposals were agreed and the one which was eventually taken up included a quota for both renters and exhibitors, starting at 10% in 1927 and increasing to 25% by 1929. It called for the abolition of 'blind booking' (see below) and recommended that the Board of Trade be given powers to keep the industry in British hands. The outcome was the *Cinematograph Films Bill in December 1927.* The final Act, in 1928, stipulated that renters and exhibitors had to take a quota of British films over 3,000 feet in length. Blind booking was made illegal by the requirement that all films had to be registered with the board of trade before they were offered for hire and no film could be registered until it could be offered to the trade. This effectively meant that an American distributor could not now sell a British exhibitor a batch of possibly unmade films a year ahead. Advance bookings were limited to six months ahead.

The advent of sound and growth

Experiments involving the synchronisation of sound with film can be traced back to Edison in the 1890's and gramophone records had been used to link film with song before the First World War. Sound on film developed with the introduction of more sophisticated equipment. After 1927, developments in this area were rapid. One example was the Vitaphone Corporation of America making shorts with the sound on disc. The demand for 'talkies' grew and the industry duly complied. The days of the silents were over.

Due to the onset of 'talkies' and the introduction of the Cinematograph Films Act, the British film industry grew rapidly during the years to 1930. As was mentioned earlier, the dominant company at the end of the 1920's was the Gaumont-British Pictures Corporation.

In addition to the growth of Gaumont, Associated British Cinemas also grew rapidly and became a major player. The Odeon emerged in the 1930's and United Artists purchased 50% of Odeons shares helping Odeon to become a formidable player in the industry.

The early 1930's also saw the arrival of J. Aurthur Rank who was set to become the major figure within the British Industry. Within a period of ten years he would control the Gaumont-British and Odeon circuits, film studios at Pinewood, Denham, Shepherds Bush and Elstree, and also a major distribution business, General Film Distributors Limited.

Ranks initial wealth was based on the family flour milling business. His initial interest in films arose from his Methodist background, with a belief that the power of film could be a positive influence in people's lives. In May 1935, Rank set up Pinewood Studios in Buckinghamshire and production began in September 1936. Rank also bought Elstree Studios in the same year.

By far the most important film production company to emerge in the early thirties was Alexander Korda's London Film Productions, formed in 1931. Korda made films that were also very popular in the United States and, as a result, investors began to take a renewed interest in film production. The American film companies, in order to be able to fulfil

17

their quotas, arranged to produce films in London. Warner Brothers and Twentieth Century Fox used British producers to make their 'quota quickies'. The quality of these films were bad and had a negative effect on the British Film Industry as a whole

From boom to slump.
By the end of 1937 the rapid growth was over. Investment had declined in the industry and British producers were faced with the choice of either making inexpensive quota films or attempting to gain a foothold in world markets with expensive productions. Expensive productions led to over-investment, mainly by insurance companies and the industry 'bottomed out'. In the light of this, the government introduced the *Cinematograph Films Act of 1938*. Quotas remained, with a new, more restrictive, system introduced to encourage more first feature films. Blind booking remained illegal. One of the outcomes of the act was to galvanise US companies into production in Britain. However, notwithstanding increased American production, the 1938 Act was seen as ineffective and counter-productive, with many film studios becoming empty or closed. Therefore, the end of the 1930's saw the British Film Industry in the doldrums with the Americans ever dominant. Then came the events of 1939, the Second World War.

The Second World War and the film industry
With the onset of the Second World War, the British government closed cinemas across the country, because of the risk of enemy aircraft and bombing. However, the effect of this was extremely negative, being both unpopular with the public and industry generally, and the cinemas re-opened soon after and remained open during the war years. As was outlined previously, the three main companies, British Gaumont, ABPC and Odeon dominated cinema owning one fifth of all

18

cinemas in Britain. Rank was to further consolidate its position during the war years. The Americans owned a limited stake in these chains.

In the light of this domination, in 1943 the government set up a committee of enquiry (Palache Committee) to investigate the growing monopoly in the British film industry. The report *Tendencies to Monopoly in the Cinematograph Film Industry,* was published in 1944, and was the first report of its kind to review the film business. It criticised the concentration of power in the combines, unfair charges by distributors, the risk to future production because of concentration of control and the danger of continuing American domination. It also called for legal limits to be imposed on the number of cinemas controlled by the major circuits. Basically, underlying the report was the notion that the government should support the independent producer.

There was also an important recommendation: that the government establish a film finance corporation to ensure the continuity of funding and establish a distribution organisation to handle independent films on merit alone. This thinking laid the foundations for what is now the Film Council in 2003 (see chapter two). The report also went as far as stating that the allocation of studio space should be decided by a tribunal, as would terms of film hire, distribution and circuit expansion. However, little action was taken apart from the circuit limitation agreement and a promise from various trade bodies to tackle their own internal problems.

Post War Years and the film industry
The election of the 1945 Labour government had a considerable impact on the film industry, as it did on the rest of society. The government supported Ranks expansion plans. Measures were also introduced to assist and protect the trade. The Granada Group expanded from 35 cinemas in 1945 to 56 in 1948 and the Essoldo chain also grew rapidly. However, in spite of expansion, the immediate post war years saw a corresponding

decline in cinema attendance. This decline was not helped by an onerous tax on films by the government in 1947, a tax of 75% on all imported films (mainly American). One person who responded positively to this tax was Rank who announced a hugely ambitious production programme in Britain. The tax and declining attendance did not stop other directors continuing film production, with Alexander Korda in particular developing London Films and acquiring other main studios. London Films produced some memorable films. In particular The Fallen Idol (1948) and The Third man (1949).

The Labour government realised, however, that the duty was not achieving the desired results and in March 1948 an Anglo-American film agreement was reached. Duty was scrapped with an increase on the amount of foreign currency to be remitted to the US (there had been continuous currency controls after the war).

In 1948, the government introduced the *Cinematograph Films Act* (of 1948) and also established the National Film Finance Corporation. Quotas were adjusted following this act, producing a less onerous situation. Initially, the NFFC had a life of five years and the government contributed £5 million. By 1951, The NFFC had spent over £5 million on films and encouraged new companies specialising in training and production.

As a result of the above, the years 1947-1948 witnessed a boom in production. Although this was welcome, at the end of the boom, Rank admitted to his shareholders that his plans had been too ambitious and over expansion had occurred with Britain still competing with a log-jam of American films. 1949 saw retrenchment after the previous years overheating and the film industry contracted significantly.

The only studio to really get it right in 1949 was Ealing with the release of Kind Hearts and Coronets, Whisky Galore and Passport to Pimlico.

The 1950's and the film industry

The end of the 1940's saw the film industry in a mess with a system of quotas in place and financing from the NFFC but still American dominance. Britain itself was still unable to break into the American market In addition to the above, the 1950's saw the emergence of a greater threat to the British film industry: the emergence of television.

During the 1950's the number of people visiting the cinema had fallen by more than half, from 27 million to 12 million. The number of cinemas also fell. This decline was due in part to the dominance of television. This was not a specifically British phenomenon as the same experience was repeated in the United States. In addition to television, radio was on the rise, with the number of listeners rising significantly.

As well as television and radio there was a problem of film supply. America had its own internal industry problems which cut short the never ending supply of feature and other films. Faced with these internal problems, largely government created, Hollywood reverted to creating better forms of visual entertainment, with the introduction of Cinemascope (20th Century Fox) and VistaVision (Paramount). Others followed suit. Gradually, and despite the cost of introducing this new visual technology, Britain followed suit.

As far as film production was concerned, the Rank organisation emerged as the leading film producer in the 1950's. Ealing studios had collapsed, notwithstanding their early successes at the turn of the decade. However, at the beginning of the 1950's, Alexander Korda's British Lion was second only to the Rank organisation in terms of studio space and facilities. Alexander Korda left the company, (responsible for The African Queen and Richard 111) and British Lion became British Lion Films Limited, with a distribution company called Lion International Films created to distribute overseas. Bryanston films was created with their films

21

distributed through British Lion. One memorable film produced at this time was Saturday Night and Sunday Morning (1959).

Therefore, a situation existed at the end of the 1950's whereby production was significant and of quality but cinemas were closing and attendances declining. In addition, the Film Finance Corporation, set up to assist the film industry, although of great help, was running at a continuous loss.

The film industry in the 1960's

In the mid 1960's the film industry in Britain was seen as being in crisis, along with the industry in other countries such as France and Italy. Declining audiences, cinemas closing, oversupply of films and the growing threat of television and, to a limited degree now, radio, all prevented investors from putting money into film.

During the late 1960's the Rank organisation was absorbed by EMI which became Thorn EMI and assumed a dominant position in the film industry, creating one of the worlds largest entertainment groups.

Film finance in the 1960's

By 1967, as much as 90% of film funding in Britain came from America. United Artists financed films such as the Beatles 'A Hard Days Night' and the James Bond films. One hundred and sixty films were made at Pinewood during the 1960's, many of them classics. These included Whistle Down the Wind, Those Magnificent Men in their Flying machines, The Ipcress File and many others. British Lion entered into a relationship with Columbia Pictures and led to such films as The Guns of Navarone, Laurence of Arabia, Doctor No and A Man for all Seasons. Due to the American led financing of films, Pinewood and other studios enjoyed a boom during the 1960's. The National Film Finance Corporation, by contrast, stood as a poor relation to the Americans.

The film industry in the 1970's

The British film industry continued to decline in the 1970's and the government reduced its subsidies to the NFFC. The American economy, in the early 1970's, was in recession and the American studios were pulling out of Britain. Hollywood itself was in crisis.

The Labour government of that period introduced a films bill designed to bolster the industry. Cinemas were being transformed with the introduction of the early 'multiplex' type cinema whereby a number of screens were grouped in one cinema. This was in spite of an oversupply of cinemas, many half empty.

The British film industry had started to restructure in the early 1970's with a series of takeovers. This, however, meant that city money was taking over all the old studios and a golden period of film production was coming to an end. In the face of this, a number of initiatives were undertaken, one being the creation of the National Film School in 1971. Between 1973 and 1981, American films began to steadily stream into England once again. Cinema audiences grew to a level not to be seen again until the year 2000. Films such as The Towering Inferno and Earthquake, big disaster movies, proved that they could pull in audiences and make a profit. The British film industry tried to follow suit producing a series of blockbusters that all flopped, notably Lord Grades Raise the Titanic. Although, at the end of the 1970's and particularly with the advent of the Thatcher government, the climate for raising film finance was difficult, new tax concessions and new distribution channels in the form of video, cable and pay TV in America were creating new markets for film.

Independent financing and the Goldcrest experience

In the face of the (never ending) difficulties faced by the film industry in Britain, counterbalanced by the growth of other opportunities in the industry, a new film company, aimed largely at producing films, Goldcrest Films, was formed in 1977. This company, during its lifecycle had a very significant impact indeed on the British film industry. The aim and vision of Goldcrest, created by Jake Eberts, was to concentrate on film development financing only. Goldcrest would bridge a gap in the industry by taking a concept, packaging that concept and selling it on to investors to fund the film production. This was a familiar practice in Hollywood.

In the early years, Goldcrest was fairly successful. Films such as Chariots of Fire were financed in 1981, working with David Puttnam. Ghandi (1982) was another film. Goldcrest also made films that were flops leading to significant losses. Bad investment decisions and crippling overheads eventually ruined the company. However, along the way, the means of financing films had been revolutionised and many new stars were created. Other film companies had followed Goldcrests example in the 1980's, Handmade Films (financed by George Harrison), Palace Pictures, Virgin and Working Title. One major problem, however, was that Goldcrest's high profile failure led to a withdrawal of investment in the film industry, from the city, once again creating problems that have dogged the industry from the beginning.

The film industry in the 1990's and the 21st Century

The lean years of the 1980's were repeated in the 1990's. However, a combination of box office hits, tax concessions by the new Labour government in 1997 and subsidies from the National Lottery transformed the industry so that, currently it is booming. The 1990's produced Four Weddings and a Funeral, The Madness of King George, Bean, The Crying game, Trainspotting, The Full Monty, The English Patient and Lock Stock and Two Smoking barrels. In box office terms, the most successful film was Notting Hill, which in 1999 grossed $350 million. Its success has started another trend of UK filmmakers raising the international appeal of their films by hiring Hollywood stars.

The dominance of the American market influenced British filmmakers to launch their own productions in America. In 1994, the distributors of Working Title's Four Weddings and a Funeral launched the film in America which was a success. The advent of new media (digital, satellite, cable) was increasing the demand for content. The 1990's also saw a select few independent producers prosper, such as Merchant Ivory Productions. However, life for independents in the current climate is still difficult. From 70 British films released in 1999, just 10 took more than $2 million at the box office and 11 British films took less than £10,000 in ticket sales. Successful independents have been Working Title with Bridget Jones Diary in 2001 and Aardman Animations, producers of Wallace and Gromit films. Cinema admissions hit a 27-year high in 2000, with more than 137 million tickets sold in the UK. This was up 3 million on 1999 due to more multiplex cinemas and Hollywood blockbusters.

Summary
It can be seen from the above brief history that the British film industry, from decade to decade, has been staggering from one crisis to another. Some of the years described above have witnessed unquestioned brilliance, only to collapse, often because of events beyond the industries control.

It is a fact that the industry has seemed to get stronger and it is fairly robust in 2002. However, British film has been dominated by America and, unlike Hollywood, the industry in Britain has always been fragmented and under-financed. Distribution has been historically weak, losing ground to America.

One of the major initiatives of the last few years has been the formation of the Film Council (2000) as a national co-ordinating body with the remit to ensure that adequate finance and training facilities exist to ensure the future growth and prosperity of the film industry in the United Kingdom.

We will be looking at the operations of the Film Council in chapter two. Following this overview, we will start to look more closely at the nature of the different areas in the film business and the jobs and training available.

-2-

Promoting Film – The Role of the Film Council

As we saw from the last chapter, the film industry has long been characterised by lack of funding and overall lack of continuity, in the process losing out to the American film industry. However, the current Labour government has recognised the various historical weaknesses, and also recognised the important fact that film is firmly established as a key part of the UK creative industries which have a collective turnover of over £60 billion per year.

The **Film Council** has been established (since April 2000) by the government as the strategic agency responsible for developing the film industry and film culture in the UK. This chapter will outline the strategy of The Film Council as formally agreed by its committee members. The chapter does not attempt to analyse the successes and failures of the Council as it is too early to attempt such an undertaking. There have, however, been criticisms emanating from certain quarters about the performance of the Film Council, not least from one of its main committee members, Alan Parker.

The Film Council's main aim is to encourage the creative industries through educational opportunity, improved access to film, excellence and innovation, in line with the objectives laid out for it by its sponsoring government department, The Department for Culture, Media and Sport (DCMS).

Since November 1999, the Film Council Board has been pursuing policies to achieve two overarching objectives:

- Developing a sustainable UK film industry
- Developing film culture in the UK by improving access to, and education about, the moving image.

The British Film Institute (BFI) which is now funded primarily by the Film Council, was restructured and refocused during 1998/1999 to deliver on the Councils cultural and educational objectives for film. The Film Councils annual budget will vary but is likely to be around £55 million per year.

The Film Council derives its money from The National Lottery and from the treasury. The Council went 'live' in April 2000, when it took responsibility for:

- The British Film Commission (promoting inward investment)
- The Arts Council of England's Lottery Film Department (investing in film production)
- The British Film Institutes Production Department (investing in film production)
- British Screen finance, a publicly supported film investment company, which has become incorporated into the Film Council.
- The British Film Institute (BFI) which is an independent body funded by the Film Council, to deliver cultural and educational opportunities for the trade.

An analysis of the current environment

The Film Council, shortly after its inception, carried out an assessment of the global environment within which the British Film Industry operates. A number of strengths and weaknesses were identified. Among the strengths which the Film Council saw as providing a solid foundation for future growth are:

- A flourishing creative community embracing writers, directors, producers and acting talent
- Strong links with creative and financial partners from Europe, North America and the rest of the world
- A competitive advantage conferred by the English language
- A tradition of innovation and creativity, notably in respect of new talent
- A highly developed infrastructure for financing, licensing and selling films internationally
- Highly skilled technicians and other crafts who attract inward investment from across the world, most especially the US
- An internationally competitive post-production industry operating at the cutting edge of new technology
- A growing number of cinema screens
- A growing domestic audience for films

However, counteracting the strengths are a number of identified weaknesses:

- An insufficient number of integrated UK companies operating across development, production and distribution
- A failure to attract sufficient finance from the financial markets or other investors
- Under capitalised production companies
- A UK distribution sector which does not prioritise British films
- An under developed entrepreneurial and business skills base
- Under resourced script development resulting in too many poor quality films being made

- A failure to capitalise upon the full range of opportunities offered by digital technologies
- A lack of investment in new talent
- A patchwork of initiatives in the English regions which collectively do not contribute sufficiently to the commercial film industry
- A continuing exodus of established talent to Hollywood
- A well developed appetite amongst audiences and exhibitors for US films
- A failure to draw upon and reflect the full social and cultural diversity of the UK

The Film Councils goal of contributing towards a genuinely sustainable British Film Industry can, it is seen, only be achieved over a number of years. The success of the industry is seen as being based on:

- The emergence of more integrated British film companies competing effectively in the global market
- A consistent flow of quality British films which attract larger audiences
- Enhanced access to private-sector finance
- More effective distribution of British films both in the UK and overseas
- A diverse and flourishing exhibition centre
- A significant and consistent level of inward investment to UK based film production
- Becoming an integral part of the European film industry
- Maintaining close trade relations with the US
- A skilled, competitive and culturally diverse workforce
- Exploiting the full potential of digital technologies

- A common purpose between the UK's publicly-funded film agencies
- Properly reflecting the cultural diversity of the UK
- Improved distribution and exhibition of a broader range of films in the UK
- Building a more film-aware audience
- Improving audience access to the UK's heritage and industry

Following this analysis, the Film Council drew up a two-stage action plan. Stage one entailed setting up a new programme for the use of public funds in order to achieve the following:

- Improve script quality
- Stimulate commercial-film making in partnership with the private sector
- Encourage creative innovation
- Improve the quality and appeal of British films
- Improve the skills of the UK's talent base
- Encourage the use of new production technologies
- Bring structural coherence to public support for film
- Reduce the existing overhead for production support in order to fund new initiatives

In addition, the Film Council undertook to further develop other initiatives already underway, such as the expansion of the British Film Commission and encouragement of film exports.

Stage two of the Film Councils Strategy, worked on through 2000, entailed developing a detailed package of policy proposals designed to encourage real structural change for the benefit of the British film

31

industry leading to an action plan to further broaden the range of films available to UK audiences.

The above represents a summary of the proposals of the Film Council. In order to achieve the objectives across the board, the Film Council has established a number of funds and units dealing with development and production of films.

The Film Development Fund

As we have seen, the Film Council identified the lack of support for script development as the biggest single problem affecting the ability of the UK industry to deliver a consistent flow of high quality films. All sectors of the industry agree that the lack of support for script development results in finished films which are too often sub-standard and subsequently wholly or partially rejected by the distribution sectors.

The Film Council has allocated £5 million per year over three years to develop scripts. This fund is overseen by industry professionals who assess and approve individual projects and slates of projects through joint venture arrangements with the private sector. The development fund is one of the largest of its kind in Europe.

In keeping with the Film Councils approach to developing UK talent, the development fund is closely linked to the Film Councils training fund for writers and development executives. Applications and pitches are welcomed from producers, writers and directors, as well as established film companies.

The Premier Production Fund

The Film Council has set up the Premier Production Fund for the development of the production sector. This fund recognises the need to offer funding at the production stage for viable high quality films at an early stage in the financing process. Committing production finance at this point will enable the production sector to leverage better terms from the private sector to complete the financing package.

The Film Council has allocated £10 million per year for three years (from the funds inception) to invest in feature film production. The fund is managed by a head of production recruited from the commercial film industry and there is an investment ceiling of £1 million per film. The fund aims to invest in 10-12 films per year.

The New Cinema Fund

The new cinema fund has an annual budget of £5 million for three years in order to support and nurture new talent and to encourage cutting edge and experimental film making of low budget and short films. A strong emphasis will be placed on the use of new technology.

In addition, a proportion of the new cinema fund will be dedicated to regional activities and identifying and nurturing emerging film talent. Applications and pitches are welcomed from individuals and organisations with talent.

First movies

A grant-funded regime supported by £1 million of lottery funds offers young people and children the opportunity to try filmmaking and display their talents. Films are shot using latest low cost technology and operate on a regional basis and a showcase will be developed for the best films.

The Film Training Fund

The Film Council sees training as the key to sustained success of the UK industry. The creativity and talent at work in the UK industry is world class. However, the maintenance of the skills base during a period of accelerated technological change is essential to retaining the UK's competitive position, both as an indigenous industry and as a magnet for inward investment.

A number of priority areas for action in the field of training have been identified. As a result, SKILLSNET (the national training organisation for broadcast, film, video and interactive media) now supports training for craftspeople and production accountants as well as health and safety training and delivery of NVQ qualification measures, with money generated by the industry backed Skills Investment Fund (SIF). The Film Council has allocated £1 million per year for three years to support training initially in the areas of scriptwriting, script editing and film development and also training for producers, business executives and distributors. See chapter 1o for a cross section of courses at all levels on offer throughout the country.

In chapter one we looked briefly at the history of the growth of the British Film Industry. It can be seen that, as the industry has experienced cycles of growth and subsequent collapse since the turn of the century, and particularly since the end of the First World War, coupled with the experience of American dominance, many lessons have been learnt. However, as has been the case for many years, government intervention is needed. This time around the government has recruited experienced professionals to advise the Film Council and, for the first time for many years, there seems to be hope that help and assistance is at hand.

There is still a great deal of debate concerning the activities of the Film Council, particularly in the regions, where some say a lot of harm is being done. However, on balance the development of the film council is seen as positive.

Having examined, generally, the history, financing and development of the film industry, it is now time to move on and look more specifically at the actual processes of filmmaking and also at the range of jobs involved.

-3-

Stages of Film Making and Film Personnel

We have seen that the film industry is complicated and a challenge for anyone who chooses to enter it, in whatever capacity. The film industry utilises large sums of money and the whole process is (or should be) highly organised and skilful. In fact, the process of making a film is rather like a highly organised military operation. So many personnel are involved, with the various stages requiring a high degree of synchronisation.

In the light of this, we need now to move away from the generalities of the film business and, bearing in mind the Film Council's emphasis on skills and training, and its overall approach to stimulating the industry, we need to focus in on the actual process of making a film and the jobs within this process. From this point on the reader will begin to gain a wider insight into filmmaking and also begin to decide which areas are of particular interest in terms of career development.

Subsequent chapters outline the various ways of getting a first foot on the career ladder by detailing courses and other opportunities available to those who wish to enter the industry.

The steps and roles in the film making process
There are three main steps in filmmaking of whichever nature, whether feature films, commercials or documentaries. These steps are as follows :

- Pre-production
- Production

- Post-production

The Pre-production stage in film making – financing a film

The pre-production stage is the stage when all of the elements in the filmmaking process are organised in preparation for the actual filming. The producer of the film first finds the story or develops the concept of the film and obtains finance. This is one of the most complicated stages, as a credible script or story has to be used to convince would-be financiers. Before looking at other aspects of pre-production we will examine aspects of financial management.

Control and sources of finance

Production accountants are very important members of a film making team. The accountants will work closely with the producer and the investors. It is their responsibility to ensure that all aspects of finance are managed. Finance rules many aspects of filmmaking as it does other industries. If the investment is not adequate then the film may never get off the ground. This maxim applies to all films whether low budget or not.

Understanding film finance management is a key to achieving success in the film business. Everything that is planned and executed is underpinned by money. In America, most studios have close links with distributors who will provide funding from the pre-production research and development stages. As we have seen, in the UK there are initiatives which are helping to bring the industry in line with the American model.

Accountants and tax specialists will explore all options to reduce the tax bill on feature films and play a very important part in the production team. It is a fact that many film producers are trained accountants and lawyers. If you wish to pursue a career in this area it will usually be necessary to pursue a course in accountancy or similar prior to entering the industry. In some cases, larger companies will advertise for trainees.

36

Sources of funding

Before film production the initial funding or investment may come from a variety of sources, distributors and TV companies, a diversity of different investors, from city institutions, banks, companies and individuals. This type of investment will require some sort of payback, particularly as there is a risk element. As we have seen, in addition to private sources, public subsidy can be awarded, particularly through the Film Council via the lottery.

In addition to the above, filmmakers may benefit from favourable loan terms. Whatever the sources of funding, budgets need to be finalised and agreed. Details of individual budgets will vary but generally the finances of a film will look like this:

Production costs (cast and crew, sets, locations, equipment, costumes etc.)	60%
Key personnel costs (stars, director, writer, Director of Photography, Producer)	15%
Overheads (Production company costs, studio rental, etc.)	12%
Other artists (Exrras, musicians, etc)	5%
Legal, financial and other professional costs	4%
Other general expenses	4%

Expenditure is divided into two areas, 'above-the-line', all agreed before the shooting for example fixed fees for personnel, and below-the-line which are changeable items such as travel, film costs etc. These are the normal conventions of business, i.e. variable and fixed costs.

See appendix 1, 'Film Finance generally' for further details about obtaining funding for making a film.

Other stages of pre-production

During pre-production the director is hired, the film is cast and the crew employed. There are numerous skills involved within the crew which will include jobs such as cameraman/woman, director of photography, production manager, production runner, production buyer, property master, gaffer (electrician) first, second and third assistant, script supervisor, boom operator, art director and set dresser.

A budget for the film and a schedule of shooting are prepared, these usually being the responsibility of the production manager, working in conjunction with accountants and other specialists.

The Production stage

This is the actual process of filming or 'shooting' the picture. It is done either on location or in a studio. Usually, the majority of key personnel are involved at this stage. This is when all of the hard work carried out at the beginning bears fruit. See chapter four for a detailed analysis of the actual process of filmmaking which will serve to highlight the stages of production along with the roles of personnel.

The Post-production stage

After shooting, the film is processed by a laboratory, edited and then completed. Editing involves not only cutting the picture but also adding the sound track, opticals (manipulation of images) titles and special effects. This particular stage can often take longer than the actual filming.

Job descriptions

The roles and responsibilities in the world of film making often overlap, as they do in other industries. This is very much dependent on the type of film being made. Feature films will usually have a much larger crew with several assistants, such as assistant producers and directors, whereas documentaries will keep the crew down to the bare minimum. We will describe the making of a documentary in a later chapter.

Few technicians have the luxury of working in one area of film making only - most will do a number of films in one year, including commercials, possibly a feature, and several independent productions. Below is a general guide to the range of jobs available in the film industry.

Scriptwriter

The origins of any feature film are based in a script, or a film treatment. A treatment is the initial source document for a film and is an interpretation of a book or some other source which is then translated into a draft script. The *scriptwriter* is the key person in this process. The treatment is then worked on and enhanced with more detailed descriptions of character and plot and the treatment is worked up into an outline script. A script is usually defined as action (picture) and sound (music). The scriptwriter, as stated, is the key person at this stage. The usual development stages which a scriptwriter will follow are:

- The initial treatment
- The production of an outline
- The production of a dialogue script
- Shooting script

The shooting script will usually involve the input of the film director who will need to be involved in the more precise planning of the shooting of each shot.

The script treatment is a very important, some would say crucial, stage as it is at this stage that funders and potential actors are sought. The treatment is the magnet for both funders and actors and others who will become involved with the film. It is for this reason that the Film Council is taking such an active role in developing this part of the industry.

The scriptwriter, or budding scriptwriter, will send the treatment to potential directors. The contact details for directors, or general contact details, are contained in chapter 9 of this book. If a director becomes interested in your treatment he or she will almost certainly be able to assist you in taking this further. The director will usually have contacts and will have worked with a production company to which he or she can introduce you.

Scriptwriters, first and foremost, need the desire and ability and talent to write. Essentially, it is the role of the scriptwriter to provide the source from which the film or documentary can be produced. The appreciation of a good potential film story is also necessary. There are various ways of studying to be a scriptwriter:

1. By obtaining existing scripts, many of which are published in book form from specialist bookshops, and studying those scripts.
2. By reading one of the many books published on scriptwriting available from specialist bookshops listed in the British Film Institute Film and Television Handbook.
3. By trying to obtain employment as a reader for a film or television production company. Readers will look and assess the potential of the masses of ideas submitted to companies and directors and it will provide the opportunity for you to study and analyse scripts and select good from bad.
4. Finally, by taking a course on scriptwriting at a film-school which employs professional scriptwriters (see chapter 10).

Once having produced a first script then you must begin the process of sending it to directors, independent companies, television companies and so on until you receive a response.

The film producer

The film producer is one of the most prominent people in the process of filmmaking. The producer of a film is very often mixed up with the film director. Whilst their roles are mutually complementary they are also very distinct. The producer of a film is one of the most important personnel controlling the organisation and finances, and is the final authority on all practical matters.

The producer will come up with the idea for the film and obtain any rights necessary, such as rights to a novel or script, or oversees the writing of an original screenplay. The producer is responsible for raising the necessary finances for the film (at the outset the seed money and later the full finance for the film). The producer will hire the director and is closely involved in casting, finding locations and hiring the crew. The producer controls the budget, making certain that the film does not overrun. The producer, in short, will put the entire package together and will monitor the day-to-day progress.

A good producer will be interested in a number of projects and will regularly come up with ideas for production. A good producer is highly disciplined and organised and has to control numerous jobs at one time. It is the case that very few people start their careers as producers, usually entering the industry in some other capacity and graduating to the role of producer.

Producers need to have a variety of interpersonal skills, be good with people (the producer/director relationship is very often strained) and have a good list of outside contacts, including film studio contacts, in order to be able to raise finance and other resources.

41

Director

The director of a film has numerous responsibilities, the main one being the responsibility for deciding how best to use the resources available to him/her. The resources are technical and artistic. The director will be in charge of directing both the actors and the camera and decide how the film will be mapped out and how best to interpret the script for the camera. The director will guide the actor's in their interpretation of a part and will tell the cameraman what kind of image he is looking for. The role of the director is of vital importance and the director needs to understand the available resources, such as cameras and lighting and the editing process. The director has to be able to conceptualise the script and visualise it Directors need to know what they want to say and how best to say it, using certain images, sounds and effects. The director has complete control of the studio and location floor and controls the film artistically, having the final say on all creative matters. The responsibilities of the producer and director will almost invariably overlap and often clash. It is very important indeed that both producer and director work well together.

Continuity - The Production manager

The production manager is responsible for the overall organisation of the picture, working under the producer. The production manager is the producer's deputy and is very actively involved in the day-to-day problems of filming. It is the production manager's job to prepare a detailed budget for shooting during pre-production and a shooting schedule based on the budget. The production manager will work very closely with both producer and director.

Once the film is at the production stage, the production manager supervises the smooth running of the shoot, and is responsible for such things as contracts being completed correctly, the hiring of equipment and obtaining permission to film in certain locations. The production manager will often act on behalf of the producer. It is the production manager's responsibility to ensure that the film comes in on time and under budget, using the resources in the most efficient manner possible.

Assistant director

There are usually three assistant directors, a first, second and third. Although called assistant directors, they work more in tandem with the production department. The first assistant will help the director, but is not the deputy, except in crowd scenes.

The first assistant will anticipate and carry out the director's practical requirements. He/she supervises the discipline and general organisation of the daily shooting schedule, prepares the call sheets, and liases with the production manager to make sure the technical needs for the following days shooting are met. The first assistant is an important link between the production department and the director, often conveying requests from one to the other. It is usual that first assistants graduate to the role of production manager as opposed to director. The first assistant will usually hire a second and third assistant to create a team. The second and third will assist the first assistant in his/her role. The second assistant will usually work more closely with the production office, preparing for the following day's or week's shooting, making sure all the resources required are available. The third assistant will work on the set, and is responsible for the artists receiving their call and ensuring they are on the set when needed.

The assistant directors are responsible for keeping a good working atmosphere on the set, and are responsible to both crew and cast. They are often a barometer of the crew's feelings, letting the director know when there are problems. The assistants are there to maximise the efficiency of the film unit and to foresee and predict problems, rectifying them before they happen.

Lighting cameraman

Although termed cameraman, this particular role can be either male or female. The person doing this job is often called the cinematographer or director of photography. Apart from the director, this person is the most creative member of the film making team. He/she will work very closely indeed with the director, and is responsible for lighting each shot, choosing camera angles, lenses and filters. The lighting cameraman/woman decides how each shot should look and how best to interpret the director's intentions. However the job does not usually involve positioning or handling the camera. This is the job of the camera operator.

Camera operator

The camera operator handles the camera for the cameraman/woman. The two will form a close-knit team, going from one production to the next, their individual styles being closely united. The operator is responsible for a smooth and efficient camera movement, and attends to the physical details of each shot.

There will often be several camera assistants. The first is called the focus puller, in charge of the actual focussing of the camera. He or she will need to collaborate smoothly with the operator. The focus puller will also need a large degree of technical knowledge.

The second camera operators assistant, called the clapper/loader is in charge of loading and unloading the camera. He or she will also fill out the camera sheets, keeping an accurate and careful record of each shot, including types of film used, the types of lens and the number of feet of film shot. The clapper loader also operates the clapperboard before each shot.

Video camera operation in a studio is a different type of work requiring different skills. Before shooting, the camera operator will read the camera script and discuss shots and angles with the director. While shooting, the operator will wear a headset to hear directions from the director or floor manager. Excellent hand-eye co-ordination is needed to position the camera focus and compose the shots at exactly the right time. Camera operators will need a practical interest in photography, lenses and lighting and the ability to compose a shot.

Sound personnel

Known as sound operators, sound recorders and mixers work in all areas of the business. In the studio they will work on the studio floor setting up and operating sound booms, microphones and loudspeakers. They can also work in the control room, where they can operate the mixing desk, tape recorders and play-in machines. They are responsible for controlling sound levels and the tonal quality of the sound. On location it can range from just one sound recordist on a videotape machine to a team of boom swingers and a sound-mixer to control the various sound levels. Sound personnel rarely work both on location and in a sound studio - the two areas are very different. People working in sound should have an interest in all aspects of sound, including music and have normal hearing.

Sound mixer

He/she is responsible for recording the sound on location and balancing the levels to make sure that they are in perspective. The sound mixer usually has an assistant, the sound recordist.

Boom handler

The boom handler will control the microphones which are hung out of view of the camera. The mixer or recordist will determine the position of the mikes.

45

Dubbing mixer

The dubbing mixer works in post-production in a sound studio. The dubbing mixer supervises the recording of additional sound, including music and special effects. He or she will obtain live effects in the studio and record dialogue that was unusable. The dubbing mixer sits on the console and decodes the appropriate level of sound, and is responsible for post-synching (matching image to sound). This particular job is highly technical and very creative, and it often takes years of experience before becoming a qualified dubbing mixer.

Editor

Though most of the editors work takes place after filming (post-production), some minor editing might go on during filming. A director sometimes consults an editor to get the best possible image from a particular shot.

The editor's job is to position the shot, choose the best angles and frames of film and cut them together. He/she is the person who determines the narrative structure of the film, by cutting, editing and assembling the picture. An editor's job is very important, as important as other key personnel such as director. The editor can make or break a picture. The editor will usually work with two assistants who collect the first prints of a film after shooting (rushes), put location sound to picture for viewing and also join the cuts together under the supervision of the editor. The assistants will maintain careful records of each shot. Often the first assistant director will assume a greater degree of responsibility than the other assistants and will work independently of the supervising editor.

Researcher

Broadcasting researchers work as part of a production team. They can be involved in developing ideas for programmes and working on them through to completion. They need to be good at finding information and contracting people to give comments and interviews. Some researchers will have a high level of knowledge in a specific area, others are more generalist and work on a wide range of programmes. Current affairs and documentaries tend to use researchers quite a lot. The feature film industry will also use researchers to check historical details.

Studio floor manager

Floor managers work in television studios. They act as a link between the floor and the director to organise and co-ordinate all the sequences of a shoot, and also have to deal with performers and technicians to make sure that they all work smoothly together.

Art department

The art department consists of the designer, art director, draughtsman, set dresser and property buyer. This is a department where training outside of the industry is absolutely necessary as well as having the talent and ability to draw, technical drawing or architecture or graphic design for example. Set dressers and property buyers should be able to interpret plans, and have the ability to find relevant items called for by the designer, especially for films which do not have a contemporary setting.

An advantage of working in the art department is that your specialism is not solely reliant on films and employment can be taken up elsewhere whilst waiting for film work.

Costume design

This department incorporates costume designers and wardrobe personnel. Formal art school training or practical training in the garment industry is really necessary. Many costume designers start in the theatre and continue to do theatre work whilst working in film. Working in collaboration with

47

the designer and the lighting cameraman is part of the job and therefore colour co-ordination and a knowledge of materials is necessary, both from a practical and budgetary viewpoint.

The costume designer's work may overflow into dressmaking and fitting and although wardrobe is responsible for ensuring that the right clothes are there in the right condition this job may be shared.

For jobs in this area, it may be useful to write to the production manager or costume designer of film companies, and other production companies and outline your qualifications and practical experience and also your desire to develop a career in this field..

Craftsmen/women

There are a number of craftsmen/women involved in filmmaking. They are as follows:

- Carpenters
- Plasters
- Painters
- Riggers
- Electricians
- Make-up
- Hairdresser
- Wardrobe
- Props
- Upholsters
- Construction manager
- Plumbers
- Scaffolders

All of the above crafts in feature films, excluding electricians, have traditionally come under the umbrella of The Broadcasting Entertainment Cinematograph and Theatre Unions as do other specialised staff such as drivers or catering staff.

There is no specific training relating to feature films for these crafts and opportunities have to be sought through trade press, word of mouth etc. See chapter 9 for the address of BECTU.

Laboratory work

Within the laboratory will be the negative cutter, colour grader, optical printer and laboratory contact.

Laboratory work is a vital part of the whole production process although now more restricted. For those with scientific leanings the job can be very rewarding. The jobs listed above are all in the higher echelons of the laboratories and are usually recruited from people who have experience in other departments. The starting points for these jobs are usually in developing, printing and cleaning for which no formal qualifications are required beyond GSCE but an interest in photography is necessary. There are several film handling courses available. See course information further on in this book for these courses. The main one in this area is run by Kodak.

Film publicity

Publicists, whether employed exclusively on a feature film and called unit publicists, or working for a company that is responsible for publicity on a number of projects, usually move from a public relations related field or from journalism. Stills photographers may be employed in the same way and come from similar backgrounds.

There can be opportunities in the publicity department of a feature film or a publicity company for runners or office juniors but you will need a good basic level of education in order to get in on the ground floor. There are a number of companies specialising in publicity, the numbers of which can be obtained from the British Film Institutes website.

-4-

Making a Short Feature Film

Having outlined the various jobs available, related to the differing stages of filmmaking, we will now take a look at the actual process of producing a short film. This will further help to place the various roles in context.

The making of a film

After the initial stages of the production process have been completed and the first days shooting schedule has been fixed, the production office will issue call sheets to those involved in the making of the film and, if location shoots are involved, a movement order, i.e. a schedule of locations and timing, will be issued. The call sheet might specify that personnel involved be at the studio at a particular stage. Trades such as make up, hairdressing, wardrobe and the relevant artists for that day will be called earlier so that they will be ready to start rehearsals as soon as possible, usually after 8.30am. The director, joining with the lighting cameraman, the camera operator and the artist can then start to choreograph the scene, working out the camera movement, dialogue and action so that the lighting cameraman can tell the chief electrician (gaffer) how he wants the lights placed.

As soon as the scene is mapped out, the grips can lay the tracks if necessary and the focus puller can start checking the various changes in focus throughout the shot and the sound crew can sort out the best positions for the microphones and boom.

The lighting may be the longest part and, if very complicated, stand- ins for the principals may be used to avoid the artists getting too hot and tired.

Rehearsals

The time has come for rehearsal. The director calls for 'action'. The first rehearsal is then underway. The rehearsal is absolutely necessary for all key personnel involved, such as cameraman and lighting crew to make all necessary adjustments before the final cut.

The first filming

After rehearsals, the director, or first assistant director is ready to say 'standby for a take-everybody quiet'. Then comes the order 'turn over' which is the signal to the sound recordist to switch on the tape recorder and report 'running' and for the camera operator to switch on the camera and when it is up to the required speed to report 'speed' at which the first assistant director orders 'mark it' to the clapper/loader. This gives the cue for the clapper /loader to get in with the clapper board, shouting out the slate and take number, bring the hinged portion down with a loud clap and withdraw. This is perhaps the most potent of all images of filmmaking and one that the public is the most familiar with.

Only after this sequence has taken place can the director order 'action' and the scene proceed up to the time that the director orders 'cut', which is the signal for everything to come to a halt.

The director will then seek the views of camera and sound crew and will make a decision as to whether to go for another take. If this is the case, the first assistant director orders 'once more please-first positions' and the whole process is repeated until everyone is satisfied. There can be many takes before a director is satisfied with a film, sometimes as many as 30.

After the various takes, the director has to decide on which take he wants printed and this information is given to the camera and sound crew so that they can make respective notes.

The notes concerning takes are eventually given to the laboratory so that they know which take to produce.

At the end of the working day, an end to shooting will be called, with the first assistant director stating 'it's a wrap'.

This call, for a wrap, does not, however, signal the end of the day for all involved in the film production. The clapper loader has to deal with the film, other involved in the control of equipment, such as the boom swinger will have work to complete, the grips pack away camera equipment and other departments will make sure that all is ready for the next days work. The script supervisor will be typing up the continuity sheets which provide information on every shot completed that day and are sent to the production office and the cutting room.

At the end of the day there will be a screening of the *rushes*. The rushes is the term used to describe what has been shot that day and assembled by the editor and his crew. The producer, director and editor will attend the filming of the rushes and also others selected by the director.

Initial stages of post- production
As we have seen, post - production means the assembling and editing of all film and sound, recording of music, creation, re-recording and mixing of sound tracks, making of graphics for titles and the processing of film in the laboratory from the developing and printing of the rushes to the making of the final prints for release to cinemas. The post-production stage is a very important part of the whole process and pieces together all of the work undertaken during the production process.

The picture negative produced from the days shoot will have been developed and printed overnight by the laboratory and prints are

53

despatched to the cutting room. The first job of *assistant editors* is to 'synch' up the rushes. This is done by placing the print of the picture and the magnetic tape in a synchroniser which is a device for running two or three pieces of sprocketed film or tape in parallel on a cutting room bench. The assistant then has to find the relevant slate and take the number on the picture and mark with a chinagraph pencil the exact frame where the hinged part of the clapperboard meets the lower part. He then has to find on the magnetic tape, listening to the voice of the clapper/loader, the same slate and take number and the sound of the clap marking this exact frame also with the china graph. The picture and sound are then put into the synchroniser in parallel and are wound onto wire spools with two lengths of 'leader' at the front with parallel start marks for the projectionist to lace up when running the rushes.

After the rushes have been viewed, the picture and sound will be sent for numbering-that is the printing of the slate number and the cumulative footage down the side of the film and tape from the clapperboard to the end of the scene. After numbering, the rushes have to be logged into a notebook.

Breaking down the rushes

The next job is for the rolls of rushes to be broken down into their separate slate numbers. These are individually rolled up and put into tins or boxes clearly labelled for easy access. The reels build up as shooting proceeds, editing takes place as the reels build up and therefore it is possible to have a rough assembly of the whole film shortly after shooting ends. There will probably be sections missing, such as special effects and certain stunts which will be shot after the main shooting and cut into the film. The first assembly of a film is usually too long but, for obvious reasons, it is better to start that way and to cut down and reduce and tighten up sequences.

The role of the editor is crucial at this stage, with the editor working very closely with the director to arrive at the finished film.

The rough cut

When the whole film has been assembled and roughly edited, all the reels of cutting copy, action and sound are called the rough cut. They are gradually fined down and tuned until the *fine cut* is reached. The fine cut is screened to the producer who will probably have a point of view, given that the producer has to consider the interests of the investors and distributors. However, at this stage, the producer has to be very tactful indeed as the first loyalty is not to the investors but to the film itself. It may be necessary for more showings of the film to be arranged before the final cut can be arrived at.

The film sound track

After the film has been completed, it will now be time to prepare the sound track. The editor and director will be instrumental here. Here a *Dubbing editor* with one or more assistants will take over the process and assume responsibility for this part of the operation right up to the stage of dubbing the film. Dubbing means the mixing together of all the sound tracks – dialogue, music and sound effects – at the right levels so that there is a balance and maximum effect is achieved.

Music

A composer will have been appointed and the music for the film considered. The principal consideration in background music is that there are no rules as such. Simple music can succeed, whereas over complicated music can fail. The opposite can be true. The judgement is very much down to the key producers of the film with the musician at the centre. The composer will complete the score and he will try it out on the director and producer.

When all are satisfied the composer will commence work. If an orchestra is used, the composer may employ a *fixer*. A fixer signs up the best instruments available at the time that the music recording theatre has been booked for the session.

The music recording will be attended by the producer, director and editor and the assistant will have marked or removed the various sections from the cutting copy. During the recording, the section of music is projected on a screen or monitor facing the conductor and the start of each section is cued in from zero with the accumulating footages also projected.

A copy of the score will also be with the *recordist or recording engineer,* who also has the responsibility for placing the various microphones for the instrument in the studio. The recording engineer is responsible for achieving the best balance possible between the instruments in collaboration with the composer. Other technicians involved in the process are the recording assistants and projectionists who screen the music sections of the film.

Sound effects
The dubbing editor will now be acquiring the sound effects for the film, either by arranging to have them specially recorded or by obtaining them from a library of sound effects.

Dubbing the film
When all the tracks have been completed and laid, the assistants will prepare a dubbing cue sheet to assist the mixer in the dubbing theatre. These cue sheets are made up for each reel and show the footage of every sound against descriptions of the picture with special sound punctuations marked. The dubbing theatre is a viewing theatre equipped for running the picture with a great many tracks interlocked to run synchronously.

Once laced up, they can be run forwards or backwards remaining in synch.

Laboratory work

When the dubbing has been completed, provided the film is scheduled for a normal cinema release, the mixed magnetic track is transferred to negative film which is sent to the laboratory for developing. Apart from the final work at the lab, there are only two other processes of post-production which concern the cutting room. The first is the design and photography of the titles and credits and the ordering and make up of opticals. Opticals are fades in the picture, mixing from one scene to the next or any other device for transition between scenes other than a straight cut.

Negative cutting and grading

The negative of the film has remained virtually untouched all this time in the laboratory, apart from logging. When the cutting copy is received at the laboratory, a negative cutter is allocated to the film whose job it is to match the negative scene by scene to the cutting copy, cutting the negative to the right length. Upon completion of the negative cutting, the film now passes to the colour grader for his assessment of each scene for colour printing. The film is now ready for a first colour combined optical print to be made. The final outcome is a show copy, suitable for public viewing.

The production processes are now complete. The final stages include all the administration such as preparation of trailers, registration and censorship and completion of accounts plus arrangements for publicity and marketing.

After reading the above synopsis of the process of film making, it should be obvious to all that it is a complex and highly organised process

57

which requires the services of a large number of people operating in a highly organised environment. Thee above description of feature filmmaking should have helped to put the various roles in context and will have shown how each key person is intrinsically linked to another within the multi-disciplinary environment.

-5-

Film Marketing and Distribution

We have seen that the personnel involved in making a film are many and varied. We have also seen, at the outset, that obtaining and managing finance is a complex operation. There is one other area of the film world that is crucial, this is the marketing and distribution of films. Without successful distribution then a film will invariably fail.

Marketing is essential, if the potential audience is to be made aware of the films existence. 'Positioning' a film – attracting particular audiences – requires particular skills. For example, communicating effectively with 18-25 year olds is a very different matter to communicating with 45 year olds. Therefore, the same films are usually packaged differently to a range of potential audiences to attract the maximum audience. It is quite common to see the contents of an advert for the same film packaged differently in two different newspapers, for example the Sun and the Guardian. This is because of the differing lifestyles and perceptions of the readers.

Big budget films will allow for a build up., or lead in period (often known as 'hype') to create interest before a film is released. In fact many millions of pounds are usually spent for big budget film in order to whet the public appetite for a film, to ensure maximum attendance. Many film-goers have commented that the actual film can quite often be a disappointment.

Most British films do not have the luxury of big marketing budgets and rely on word of mouth, awards and good reviews to attract audiences.

One other marketing tool has opened up new horizons – the internet. One such film which achieved success off the back of the internet was the Blair Witch Project, which produced huge profits following pre-release publicity over the internet. It is true to say that the internet may continue to open up new opportunities for filmmakers. However, expertise in marketing generally and a good distribution deal are the keys to success.

The potential launch time of a film is very important. This can depend on the season, what other films are being launched, school holidays and so on. Some British films are now released in the US before being shown to the home market. This can be a risky strategy but the potential size of the American audience, and the power of the media can help to build a film's reputation before it is released in the UK and Europe.

Box office takings provide the most visible source of revenue, the first week being crucial to many films. The marketing campaign is usually developed months in advance. However, this is sadly not the case for many British films, mainly due to lack of access to fiancé and also to experienced film marketers. As we saw in chapter two, the Film Policy Review Group has recommended support in this area.

When a film is in development and production it is a 'prototype' that can be altered relatively easy. Once produced, it is a product which has to be sold to the widest range of potential purchasers. Effective distribution is most certainly the key to this. If the film already has distribution, and the distributors are satisfied with the end product, the distribution process will commence.

The distribution process
The following steps are central to the distribution process:

- The film is contracted by the distributor
- A decision is taken about the number of prints for release

- The release timing is agreed, together with the geography of distribution
- Trailers of the film are made, any appropriate publicity materials developed and advertising booked
- Local and national promotional events and partnerships are arranged. For example, a major film will have tie-ins with other companies, such as Macdonald's and Burger King
- The prints of the films are delivered (the actual distribution process)

For each distribution project, a wide range of skilled personnel will be involved carrying out the following tasks:

- Selling the film to cinemas – persuading the management to give the film an early showing
- Ordering the optimum number of (expensive) prints, and then physically producing high-quality prints for distribution – a process know as print production

When a distributor agrees to take on a film, a budget will be agreed that will reflect the nature and potential profitability of the film. Many factors are involved in predicting film profitability:

- Perceived income from cinemas
- US box office takings (if relevant)
- Audience research findings
- The stars and their appeal
- The appeal of the director and crew
- Level of certification

- Timing of release
- Number of prints available and the distributors experience.

All of the above are likely to affect profitability. Broadly speaking, to make a profit a film has to return at least two-and-a-half times the production costs.

We should look in more depth at some of the above factors, as expanded upon below.

Audience research
This is becoming increasingly important. Before a film is released nationally, the distributors are likely to 'test the product' with different audiences. In addition to preview screenings there are often sophisticated focus groups. Reviews are also taken into consideration, but may be ignored if the market research is positive. Negative feedback may affect the breadth of distribution or even result in the film going straight to video.

Cast and crew
Some stars, and the director, will guarantee an audience, particularly a star name. This is not always good for the quality of the film as in many cases the star name just does not fit the actual role and can seem quite incongruous. However, people are drawn by stars.

Classification
The distributor will submit the finished film for classification and pays for it to be assessed. The outcome can affect a films earning power considerably and will certainly influence the marketing and advertising strategy.

Timing of release

For some films this is very obvious. However, some other films require more careful calculation to assess the competition and other factors at a particular time.

Many of the colleges and universities outlined in chapter ten offer courses in business and marketing. Usually, it is after taking a course leading to a qualification that people move into the film business in order to train to become specialists.

-6-

Animation

Animation in the year 2002 is very sophisticated indeed and has grown into a very profitable sector. The name Walt Disney automatically springs to mind. There are many courses in existence specifically teaching the art and skill of animation, which will be outlined later. Animation – whether produced by the traditional well-known method of drawings, with models, or whether produced, as often is the case nowadays, with very sophisticated computer systems – is a very costly and labour intensive business. For example 30 minutes of animation, TV animation, may cost £350,000. Animation series may cost between £6000-£10000 per minute. And programmes can take many months to make.

However, it is the case that animation is becoming more popular as a form of entertainment and it can be marketed globally with greater ease as it 'travels well'. Animation has a long shelf life, dating far less quickly than other medium. There are regular showings of 1930's animated cartoons on TV and cinema with no sign of diminishing popularity.

If an animation production company gets it right, the long-term results can be very significant indeed. However, there are enormous risks. So therefore any undertaking has to be handled professionally and with great skill.

Similarly with film, as we have seen, technological developments and the increasing need for product from the ever increasing army of TV stations, have encouraged new animators to challenge some of the older, more traditional, ways. A new wave of adult animation has reduced costs through clever scripting and other devices. Commissioning editors and schedulers in broadcasting are starting to become more flexible in their approach to funding and broadcasting. The reason is that animation can be very popular and ratings can justify decisions.

Animation generally

The UK animation industry leads the way in creative and artistic talent in this sector. A diversity of products include:

- Commercials
- Music promotion videos
- Children's programmes
- Feature films
- Adult comedy
- Adult series
- Adult drama
- Games
- Multimedia

Animation can be divided into two quite distinctive areas, although there is a lot of crossover. There is the traditional hand drawn 'cel' animation, the type most popularly associated with Walt Disney (the original). Every movement and facial expression is drawn and then transferred onto a clear cellulose for filming.

Between 12 and 25 drawings will be consumed every second, and up to 25000 drawings required for a half hour episode. Another development of the traditional approach, as typified by Wallace and Gromit is the clay animation and model animal characters such as those from Cosgrove Hall. There is still painstaking attention to detail but by manipulating models as opposed to drawings.

Computer animation is becoming ever more dominant with increasingly more sophisticated software coming into the market place. This sector can be very expensive and time consuming – with recent feature films using 400 state of the art computers. The challenges with computerised software are significant, as computers still cannot produce the same results as human beings. However, techniques are developing very fast and it is probable that computers will replace more traditional forms as time marches on.

Many new productions are now taking advantage of opportunities to mix cel or model animation with computer generated additions.

Jobs in the industry

A wide variety of people are employed within the modern animation industry. We have already seen that the film industry employs a very wide variety of personnel essential to bringing a film into being. The animation industry is similar. Far from the traditional idea of one person and their drawing board, again popularised by Walt Disney, there is an increasing emphasis on teamwork and multi-tasking. As production lead-times increase and budgets have to be managed, it is cost effective if people can move between projects at any one time. There are still plenty of people who work alone, with traditional animation requiring long hours of concentration. However, this is offset by the need to achieve goals within tight deadlines.

The following are some of the job titles to be found in the animation sector: After having read the previous chapters on film, many of the jobs will fall into place without further description:

- Animation Director
- Art Director
- Audio Producer

- Cel painter
- Character designer
- Clean up artist
- Designer
- Editor
- Graphic Designer
- Model Maker
- Music Composer
- Producer
- Rostrum Camera person
- Special Effects Animator
- SFX Rostrum Cameraperson
- Tracer
- Animator 2D-3D
- Assistant Animator/In Between
- Background Artists
- CD-Rom Producer
- Checker
- Colourists
- Dubbing Co-coordinator
- Games Developer
- Key Animator
- Model Set maker
- Post-Production Co-coordinator
- Production manager
- Set Maker
- Scriptwriter

- Storyboard Co-coordinator
- Web Designer

There are also a variety of lesser know, but equally important, jobs:

- Administrator
- Human Resources manager
- International Sales advisor
- Rights Specialist lawyer
- Specialist Accountant
- Fundraiser
- Investment Advisor
- Marketing Director
- Runner
- Studio Manager

It can be seen from the above, that the whole process of producing an animated film is every bit as complex as producing a feature film. In many cases, the process is far more time consuming. However, the business of animation is booming with the industry very positive about the future. International ventures are becoming more commonplace. There is potential for long-term earnings and there are added advantages, for example:

International sales – animation travels well and can be dubbed easily into many languages
Licensing and marketing – characters can become sought after brands which can be used to sell a vast array of merchandise, producing money for the animation company through licensing agreements.

Videos- the children's market in particular lends itself to video production. Sales, rental or archive material can produce huge revenues.

Compilation – the material can be reworked and used in different ways to produce additional income.

Financing animation

We saw with feature films that financing is never easy and quite often investment will come from a wide range of sources. Animated films, unless very short, are expensive and money often comes from the big studios. Disney has dominated the market for many years but other studios are getting in on the act. DreamWorks, Universal and Fox are increasingly active. Aardman (Wallace and Gromit) have made their first full-length feature film with help from overseas. Budgets of $10 million are not uncommon so it is obvious that a major player is needed for support in animated ventures of any significance.

Making an animated feature

As with feature films, there are a number of clear steps involved in the production of an animated film. They are as follows:

- Original story idea, based around a central character, sold to a production company or an international distribution company which supplies production finance
- The script is developed
- Animators developed the characters and backgrounds to fit the feel of the production
- Actors chosen for the voice of each character
- Animators produce work in line with storyboards/time-plans
- Sound track recorded in 'sound dead' booth

- Detailed design check on drawings for international target markets
- Continuing research to ensure that background looked OK
- Animatic – where panels of the storyboards are scanned into a computer to give a 'rough cut' of the show
- After a number of the adjustments, the detailed animation built to produce moving colour footage with voices
- Final draft viewed frame-by-frame
- List of retakes made. To be shot and dropped in later
- Final film edited to required length.

You can see from the above that the making of an animated film is a long and complex expensive business requiring a large number of people working together as a team.

The process is similar to feature film making, in that the whole effort is like a military operation with very clearly defined job descriptions. The main difference is in the sequence of events.

Training

Training in the animation industry is at the top of the agenda for many industry specialists. Recruiting and developing people who can apply a mix of craft, technical, interpersonal and business skills is a difficult task. Some of the UK's leading companies have become involved in the provision of relevant, practical training. The Bristol Animation Course is perhaps the best example of this, supported by a group of industry specialists, who teach on the courses and also provide supervised work experience. Its aim is to develop talented but 'raw' animators. Students work an eight-hour day, five days a week and quickly learn about the demands of the industry. Another course, which has evolved for similar reasons, is the London Animation Studio, based at the St Martins School

71

of Art in London. This course concentrates on drawn and computerised animation, and in six months aims to develop industry standard skills which should make individuals more marketable. It is open to a diversity of people including those who already work in the industry.

During the Bristol course, students are assessed on a variety of attributes, including:

- Observation/characterisation
- Movement/ animation
- Staging/editing/storyboarding
- Computer skills
- Attitude to work

Employers are keen to support training that develops a range of skills needed by the industry. Skillset professional qualifications have been designed to incorporate these and a number of assessment centres have been established. Attributes sought after in these centres include:

- The ability to communicate ideas clearly
- Persuasiveness
- Patience
- Attention to detail
- Lateral thinking
- Ability to work under pressure
- Numeracy/financial ability
- Fundraising/talking to investors

Areas of particular skills shortages have been identified for scriptwriters, producers, storyboarders and layout artists.

Other training and development opportunities of interest include the following:

The British animation training scheme

Established in the mid 1990's, funded by skillset, CARTOON and the industry, 12 people working within the sector are selected each year to attend on a day release basis.

Finding out more

The Animation UK Directory – published annually by Venture publishing, in association with BECTU, contains information about:

- Specialist production companies, including special effects, multi media, games designers etc;
- People who work in all areas of the industry with names and contact details;
- Relevant service providers, including equipment hire and sales, specialist consultants and agents
- European production companies
- Other useful information

Animation UK also publishes an industry magazine. Visit their website www.animationuk.com.

-7-

Commercials and Documentaries

Commercials

One other important aspect of filmmaking that we should explore is the production of commercials. Commercials are usually either shown on television or the cinema. However, both are still made on 35mm film and therefore should be viewed as mini feature-films. What distinguishes the feature from the commercial is that the commercial is usually a lot more expensive to produce, in relative terms.

Advertising agencies

Commercials originate in advertising agencies. Commercial production companies always look to advertising agencies for their livelihoods. Agencies are powerful players and will usually write the scripts, commission the whole production and, having usually supplied the finance, own the copyright and material. Agencies will act on behalf of their clients whose products or services they have been commissioned to advertise and the use of commercials may be only part of a wider campaign by a company. Because production costs are so high along with television time the whole process of commercial making is thorough in order to ensure that the end product is as effective as possible.

Commercial production

Commercials production companies are quite often fairly small and usually revolve around one or two very talented film directors. The actual preparation, setting up, scheduling and shooting of a commercial is virtually the same for a feature film except that the overall schedule is more likely to be measured in days rather than months. This is because the running time of the average commercial is a lot less than the average feature film.

There is one other difference which is important. In the case of features, the whole organisation to make the film will probably have started from nothing. The assembling of the key players will evolve as the pre-production stage commences. In the case of a commercial production company which depends on continuity of work, the basic company structure is permanent. This will include one or more producers or directors, a production manager, accountants, secretaries and runners. Some companies have their own film and video editing facilities, but many use outside facilities companies.

As with feature films, the design, camera, sound and the rest of the production department will have been engaged on a freelance basis for a single or series of commercials.

The way in to commercials

One way to discover the most active agencies and the most favoured production companies is to study the trade papers like Campaign, Broadcast, Marketing Week or Marketing and then write to the agencies and/or production companies that feature most strongly.

In addition to job opportunities similar to feature films and the possibility of administrative jobs in production companies, there are also a number of jobs in the post-production of commercials available, as below.

- On line editor
- Assistant editor
- Recordists

- Recording engineers
- Recording assistants

Working in commercials is very hectic, the whole process moving at a faster pace than feature filmmaking. Working in commercials can be a stepping-stone to film production and it is well worth commencing a career in this field. However, there is also enormous pressure so make sure that you thrive on stress.

If you are keen to work in this sector then make sure that you study the technical press (see chapter) to find out the advertising agencies, production companies and directors who are most active and approach them in the first instance via the directories.

Working in documentaries
Screenings of documentaries fall mainly into two separate areas, theatrical and non-theatrical. Theatrical entails showing a documentary in cinemas, on television or by the sale or rental of videocassette. Non-theatrical entails showing a documentary to non-paying audiences, either specially invited or through free or nominal rental or sale, usually via film or video libraries to schools, universities or any specialist organisations in industry or other professional groups.

Producing documentaries
The production of documentaries is fairly evenly divided between film and video. The deciding factor will be the size of the intended audience. However, the cost of videotape as opposed to film and the versatility of video equipment will also be a major factor.

The subjects of documentaries
The major theatrical subjects for documentaries are:

- travel
- adventure
- wild-life
- science
- art
- sport
- current affairs
- social issues

Although the above all fall into the theatrical category, they can also be instructional and overlap with non-theatrical documentaries, such as:

- teaching
- sales
- propaganda
- recruitment
- public relations
- safety

There is one major difference in the two areas and that is that films made for non-theatrical audiences have been sponsored by the relevant interested party who wishes to put the particular message across to as wide an audience as possible.

Jobs in documentaries
We have already looked at the range of jobs available in the film industry and seen how they fit into the overall making of a film. The job titles relating to documentaries are similar:

- Scriptwriter
- Researchers
- Producer
- Production manager
- Director
- Assistant director
- Unit manager
- Cameraman
- Camera assistant
- Electrician
- Sound recordist
- Boom swinger
- Editor
- Assistant editor

The above roles are relevant to film and video. However, the production processes will differ. The editing process, for example, is different with video as opposed to film.

If you are keen to get into the production of documentaries on film or video, the same advice applies as to film or commercials. Video production is specialised and it could be that you will need to gain relevant basic experience in this area to achieve initial success when job hunting.

Research in appropriate directories is the starting point then approaching the companies listed in these directories, with your C.V. Again, a course of higher education or relevant short courses will greatly assist you in this process.

-8-

The Facilities Sector

The facilities sector supplies a wide range of specialised technical services to a range of media companies. This sector is very well established in the United Kingdom and is very competitive. It is a fact that almost every new production will call on the services of one or more aspects of the facilities sector, including broadcast television, commercials, feature films, promotional videos, studios, the corporate sector and so on. Although the sector is competitive and much work goes to television and commercials the film industry generally calls upon the services of the sector.

Facilities companies supply all types of technical backup, such as camera equipment and crews, film-processing laboratories, edit suites and editors and also audio services. The sector has grown in response to the growth of independent production companies and deregulation of large broadcasters. With expanding need there has developed a supply sector. The main advantage of utilising the facilities sector is that the companies offer trained staff and technology for short-term use, thereby overcoming the obstacle of expensive employment costs.

Opportunities in the facilities sector

Recruiters are particularly keen to attract people with well-developed interpersonal skills. Customer services skills are in demand at every level. If an individual also has a high level of technical expertise then this is a distinct advantage.

Although there are some big players within the facilities sector, including BBC Resources, The industry is largely made up of small specialist companies. The number of employees will vary depending on the size of the company.

Skills and personality factors required

Many people join facilities companies at the start of their careers and develop the relevant technical skills on the job, so to speak, sometimes supported by specialised off-site training. At early recruitment stages, managers will be looking for:

- Proven technical ability
- Knowledge of IT
- Awareness of the commercial environment
- An open, customer friendly approach
- Good time management skills
- Flexibility about working hours.
- Good general business skills
- A genuine enthusiasm for the industry

The industry is in permanent need of well-trained and motivated staff and there are a variety of jobs on offer:

- On-line editors
- Off-line editors
- Telecine operators
- "D Graphics animator
- 3D Graphics animator
- Graphics designer

82

- Audio engineers
- Audio assistants
- VT Operator
- Quality operator
- Transmission engineer
- Camera operator
- Studio VT assistant
- Vision mixer
- Lighting supervisor
- Sound recordist
- Engineer
- Electrician
- Operations manager
- Facilities manager
- Studio manager

There are also jobs on the business side, including:

- Contracts administration
- Bookings assistant
- Sales and marketing director
- Managing director
- Reception
- Financial manager
- Business development executive

The main entry job within the facilities sector is that of 'Runner'. As a runner you will get many opportunities to show off your potential skills and also your enthusiasm. In an independent facilities house, you could expect the following type of career progression, if you have talent and personal skills:

Runner – VT Operator – Editor's assistant – Junior editor.
(2yrs)

Editors can earn a large amount of money, as can other jobs within the industry. The facilities sector is a very good place to commence a career in film generally.

Organising some work experience where you can get a feel for the industry would be invaluable, and gaining experiences in several different companies would help more. The companies, together with their specialisms, are listed in trade directories, such as The Production Guide Kays UK production Manual, Kemps Film, TV and Video Handbook, and The Knowledge. Once you have decided on the filed you wish to specialise in you should apply to the relevant company, sending a C.V emphasising your strong points.

Having a degree would certainly be useful. This may help you and give you a better chance than those without degrees. Students generally gain interpersonal skills during their studies and are often considered to be stronger candidates.

The majority of facilities companies can be found within the Soho area of London, although there are a number of the larger ones spread around Greater London. Around 25% of the companies are in other regions of the U.K.

Training and education
Some colleges and universities have well-established links with employers and are careful to ensure that their syllabus includes many marketable

elements. By contacting the employers and the colleges that you are interested in, you should be able to develop a shortlist of possible courses. Full time courses are listed in Media Courses (2002) and a wide range of short courses in Media and Multimedia Short Courses. Both are published by the British Film Institute and should be available in libraries. Skillset Professional Qualifications will be relevant to many jobs in this sector. Read chapters 9 and 10 for more information about courses.

Finding out more

Televisual – published by Centaur Communications is a trade magazine read by the facilities community. In September of each year it publishes an overview of the industry, nominating the best companies. *Broadcast,* published by EMAP, has a dedicated facilities section in each magazine and useful occasional specialist supplements. *The Production Show*, held in London each year (usually in March), is the best showcase for current available technology with many relevant companies exhibiting.

-9-
Further Information

So far, we have looked at the film industry, including the animation sector plus commercials and documentaries and have outlined jobs within these areas. We have also looked briefly at the actual making of a film, placing these various jobs in context. Outlined below are some useful trade associations and publications through which you may gain useful information that will help you find out more about the industry and specialised areas. In addition, in the next chapter there is a list of short and long courses should you wish to take a course of further education.

Trade associations, guilds, unions, societies and support organisations.

The film and media industry generally is supported by a broad network of associations, trade unions and guilds, which act on behalf of their membership. A selection of the most useful is listed below.

Advertising, Film and Videotape Producers Association

28 Noel Street
London W1V 3RD
020 7434 2651
www.afvpa.com

This organisation represents the interests of producers of commercials, and has negotiated agreements with the relevant unions. The AVFPA is also a member of the commercial film producers of Europe.

Amalgamated Engineering and Electrical Union (AEEU)
Hayes Court
West Common Road
Bromley
Kent BR2 7AU
www.aeeu.org.uk

The AEEU is a large multi trades union with approximately 1000 members involved in film and TV production.

British Film Commission (BFC)
10 Little Portland Street
London W1W7JF
www.britfilcom.co.uk

Now part of the Film Council the BFC is supported by government funding, the BFC promotes the UK as an international production centre and provides support for those filming in the UK.

British Film Institute
21 Stephen Street
London W1P 1PL
020 7255 1444
www.bfi.org.uk

The national agency for conserving film and broadcast. The BFI has a library open to the public and also offers research.

Broadcasting, Entertainment, Cinematograph and Theatre Union
(BECTU) 111 Wardour Street London W1V 4AY 020 7437 8506
www.bectu.org.uk

BECTU covers all technical production staff in broadcasting, film and independent production. It has agreements for these sectors and offers members representation, employment, legal and taxation services. It publishes a regular journal, 'Stage, Screen and Radio' and runs a student link up scheme for people intending to build a career in the industry. Membership provides a range of opportunities to establish contact in the industry and to gain up to date information from the journal. Students researching relevant projects will also have access to relevant advice and help from BECTU. Students and new graduates are offered discounted membership rates.

The BECTU Black Members Sub-Committee was set up to help and support members of Afro-Caribbean origin or anyone who may suffer discrimination in the workplace.

British Academy of Film and Television Arts (BAFTA)
195 Piccadilly
London W1V OLN
www.bafta.org

Bafta promotes high standards in film and TV production and has an annual awards ceremony. It holds extensive programmes of lectures, seminars etc.

British Interactive Multimedia Association (BIMA)
5-6 Clipstone Street
London W1P 7EB
020 7436 8250
Email enquiries@bima.co.uk

The trade body for the multimedia industry, it publishes a directory of members, regular newsletters and arranges a series of industry meetings.

The Moving Image Society (BKSTS) 63-71 Victoria House, Vernon Place,
London WC1B 4DA 020 7242 8400 www.bksts.demon.co.uk

This organisation organises regular meetings and demonstrations of new equipment and techniques and runs training courses. BKSTS also organises a biennial conference and specialist seminars.

British Screen Finance
10 Little Portland Street
London W1W 7JF
Email info@britishscreen.co.uk

British Society of Cinematographers (BSC)
11 Croft Road
Chalfont St Peter
Gerrards Cross
Bucks SL9 9AE
O1753 888052
Email Britcinematographer@compuserve.com

The BSC arranges meetings, film shows etc.

Broadcasters Audience Research Board (BARB)
Glenthorne House
Hammersmith Grove
London W6 OND
020 8471 9110

BARB produces statistical information which is used to calculate the ratings.

Broadcasting Standards Commission (BSC)
7 The Sanctuary
London SW1P 3JS
020 7223 0544

The BSC is the statutory body for both standards and fairness in broadcasting.

Community Media Association
15 Patemoster Row
Sheffield
S1 2BX
0114 279 5219
www.commedia.org.uk

Provides training and holds conferences and events.

CSV Media
237 Bentonville Road
London N1 9NJ
020 7278 6601
Email information@csv.org.uk

Part of the national charity Community Service Volunteers, CSV Media specialises in social action broadcasting, media support services and media training.

Directors Guild of Great Britain
Acorn House
314-320 Grays Inn Road
London WC1X 8DP
020 7278 4343
www.dggb.co.uk

Represents the interests and concerns of director in all media. It seeks to maintain high standards in the film, television and theatrical media.

Film Council
10 Little Portland Street
London W1W 7JF
www.filmcouncil.org.uk

The Film Council plays a leading role in leading the development of the British Film Industry.

Guild of British Animation
26 Noel Street
London W1V 3RD
020 7434 2651
Email afvpa@easynet.co.uk

Represents the interest of British animation companies

Guild of British Camera Technicians
5/11 Taunton Road
Metropolitan Centre
Greenford
Middlesex
UB6 8UQ
020 8578 9243

The main aim of the Guild is to represent and further the professional interests of technicians working with motion picture cameras.

Guild of British Film Editors
Travair, Spurlands End Road, Great Kingshill, High Wycombe, Bucks HP15 6HY. 01494 712313.
Aims to increase the recognition of film and sound editing as part of the creative and artistic aspects of film production.

International Visual Communications Association (IVCA)
Bolsover House
5/6 Clipstone Street
London W1P 8LD
020 7580 0962
www.ivca.org

IVCA is the professional trade association representing the interests and needs of the visual communications user or supplier. It has over 1500 members representing programme producers, commissioners, users, in-house units, facilities, manufacturers and others.

Music, Film and Video Producers Association (MFVPA)
26 Noel Street
London W1V 3RD
020 7434 2651

The MFVPA represents the major music video companies. It has an agreement with BECTU.

PACT (Producers Alliance for Cinema and Television)
45 Mortimer Street
London W1N 7TD
020 7331 6000
www.pact.co.uk

PACT serves the film and independent TV production sector and is the UK contact point for international co-production or co-financial partners and distributors. The monthly PACT magazine is useful as a source of information about the independent sector. PACT also runs an industrial relations service which provides information on standard agreements and contracts, and negotiates with the relevant unions.

Production Managers Association (PMA)
Ealing Studios
Ealing Green
London E5 5EP
020 8758 86999
www.pma.org.uk

Provides training job opportunities and support for experienced production managers.

Scottish Screen
249 West George Street
Glasgow
G2 4QE
0141 302 1700
www.scottishscreen.demon.co.uk

A government backed body encouraging film development and education in Scotland.

Sgrin-Media Agency for Wales
The Bank
10 Mount Square
Cardiff Bay
Cardiff CF1 6EE
029 2033 3304
www.sgrinwales.demon.co.uk

The Welsh national information centre for European audio-visual funding and policy in Wales. It promotes the EU action programme for the audio-visual industry.

94

Skillset
103 Dean Street
London W1V 5RA
020 7534 5300
www.skillset.org

The national training organisation for TV, radio, film, video and interactive media. Recognised by the government as the voice of the industry in training. Skillset operates at a strategic level to improve training and education policy on provision.

Women in Film and Television
6 Langley Street
London WC2H 9JA
020 7240 4875
Email wftv@org.uk

Professional membership organisation for women working in the film and TV industries. Has an annual awards ceremony and campaigns on behalf of its members.

The Writers Guild of Great Britain
430 Edgeware Road
London W2 1EH
020 7723 8074
Email tostia@wggh.demon.co.uk

The writers union, providing support and training for its members.

Specialist Film Industry Organisations
In addition to the above, there are a number of other specialist organisations associated with the film industry. The major players are listed below.

The Production Guild
C/O Sargent-Disc Ltd
Pinewood Studios
Pinewood Road
Iver Heath
Bucks
SL0 ONH
01753 657167

Guild of Location managers
C/O The London Film Commission
20 Guston centre
Regents Place
London NW1 3JH
020 7387 8787

British Special Effects Guild
Box 23 Shepperton Studios
Studios Road
Shepperton
MiddlesexTW17 OQD
01932 572631

Association of Motion Picture Sound
28 Knox street
London W1H 1FS
020 7402 5429

British Film Designers Guild
9 Elgin Mews South
London W1P 7PJ
020 7286 6716

First Film Foundation
9 Bourlet Close
London W1P 7PJ
020 7580 2111

(A charity which exists to help new British writers/producers and directors based in the UK and Ireland, to make their first film. Offers impartial practical advice and several programmes for training and development)

New Producers Alliance
9 Bourlet Close
London WJP 7PJ
020 7580 2480

(A membership organisation for producers, directors and scriptwriters which produces a directory of members and suppliers)

Film Education
020 7976 2291
www.filmeducation.org

(offers cross-curricular programmes designed to improve understanding of the film industry)

The Short Film Bureau
01273 2355525
www.shortfilmbureau.com

(Offers help to assist film-makers to get their work shown commercially)

British Council Film, TV and Video Department
11 Portland Place, London W1N 4EJ. 020 7389 3065

Film Four
76-78 Charlotte Street
London W1P 1LX

London Film and Video Development Agency
114 Whitfield Street
London W1P 5RW
020 7383 755

NESTA
33 Throgmorton Street
London EC2N 2BR

The Northern Ireland Film Commission
21 Ormeau Avenue
Belfast
BT2 8HD
02890 232444
www.nifc.co.uk

Useful Publications
Magazines and journals

Many of the publications listed below can be found in specialist libraries. Alternatively, the larger newsagents will order them on your behalf.

Animation UK
News about the growing animation industry

Ariel
The BBC in-house magazine

AW Magazine
Up-to-date information non the audio-visual business.
Direct
The newsletter of the Directors Guild of Great Britain.

Eyepiece
Introduced by the Guild of British Camera Technicians, it is also full of relevant information for aspiring film makers

Image Technology
Magazine of the Moving Image Society. Useful for anyone planning a technical career in film.

Moving Picture International
Provides an insight into the international film, TV and Video Industry. Only published during festivals.

Production Solutions
For people working in TV and film production, with an emphasis on technology, film issues and training.

Screen International
Invaluable for aspiring film-makers, it contains interviews and features.

Reference Books
The books listed below are a selection of useful reference works. They can be obtained from bookshops or specialist or business libraries. Check with publishers for prices.

Animation UK (Venue Publishing)
64-65 North Road, St Andrews, Bristol BS6 5AW. 0117 942 8491
The directory of the animation industry

BFI Handbook (BFI)
21 Stephen Street
London W1P 2LN
020 7255 1447

Contains facts and figures and addresses and contacts within the industry.

The Creative Handbook (Variety Media Publications)
34-35 Newman Street
London W1P 7FB
020 7436 8626

A-Z of Britain's Film, TV, Radio and Theatre Directors.

Directors Guild Directory (Directors Guild of Great Britain)
15-19 Great Titchfield Street
London W1P 7FB
 020 7436 8626

Directors and Producers Directory (BECTU)
111 Wardour Street
London W1V 4AY
020 7437 8506

Directory of British Film and TV Producers (PACT)
45 Mortimer Street
London W1N 7TD
020 7331 6000

Directory of International Film and Video Festivals (British Council)
11 Portland Place, London W1N 4EJ. 020 7389 3065

The IVCA Business Media Handbook (IVCA)
Bolsover House
5/6 Clipstone Street
London W1 8LD
020 7580 0962

The essential guide to the corporate visual communications industry, providing facts, figures and contacts.

Kays UK Production Manual (KAYS)
8 Golden Square
London W1R 3AF
020 8749 1214

A comprehensive manual of people and organisations in the production side of film. Contains thousands of names and addresses.

Kemps Film, TV and Video Yearbook (Variety Media Publications)
34-35 Newman Street
London W1P 3PD
020 7637 3663
Long established directory of the film and television production industries in most countries.

The Knowledge (Benn Business Information Services)
Riverbank House
Angel Lane
Tonbridge
Kent TN9 1SE
01732 362666
A comprehensive guide to the products and services of the UK film, TV and Video industry.

The Media Guide (Fourth Estate)
020 7727 8993

A source of reference for anyone planning to work in the industry.

The Production Guide (Emap Media)
33-39 Bowling Green Lane
London EC1R ODA
020 7505 8000

Annual details of technical contacts, services and equipment.

The White Book
01932 572622
International production directory

The Art of the Deal
Dorothy Viljoen PACT
Comprehensive guide to business affairs for film and TV producers.

-10-

Guide to Courses and Colleges Offering Courses

It is important before you undertake a course to make sure you find out whether it has some legitimacy and carries some weight with people in the industry. It is also very important to make sure that you choose a course that is relevant to what you want to do after you have finished. It is no good, for example, choosing a highly theoretical course in film history if you intend to embark on a career in sound or lighting. It is always necessary to receive the right advice before you commit yourself.

The courses listed below are all further education courses and short courses and are highly practical. There are many courses that are theoretical but you will need to obtain university and higher education handbooks to determine the whereabouts of such courses.

For up to date information concerning the courses listed below you will need to contact the school concerned.

The courses are normally two years long and will often incorporate an industrial placement. The entry requirements are usually 4 GCSE's grades A-C, a BTEC or SCOTVEC National Diploma or Certificate or their equivalent. As with many courses, exceptions are made for mature students with no formal qualifications.

The first section below lists a cross section of specialist film related subjects, with the appropriate college listed underneath. For contact details of the college concerned you should look in section two which lists a broad cross section of colleges and universities in the United Kingdom offering film courses. However, given that there are also many undergraduate and post-graduate courses on offer the colleges listed below represent only a small cross section of further education courses available.

For a comprehensive guide to all media courses, 'Media Courses UK' can be purchased from the British Film Institute. Price: £13.99. Alternatively, this information is now on line at the British Film Institute web site.

(1) Specific courses in film and film related disciplines

ACCOUNTANCY

BA (Hons) Accountancy and Film Studies (Modular)
Bolton Institute of Higher Education

ANIMATION

Animation
Westminster Kingsway College

Animation and Multimedia
Tower Hamlets College

Animation Assistant Course
British Animation Training Scheme

BA (Hons) Animation
Brighton College of Technology

BA and BSc (Hons) Animation
University of Glamorgan

BA (Hons) Animation
University of Lincolnshire and Humberside
Surrey Institute of Arts and Design
University of Wales Newport
University of Wolverhampton

BA (Hons) Animation and Illiustration
Southampton Institute

BA (Hons) Animation, Media and Society
Northbrook College

BA (Hons) Another subject with digital animation
London College of Music and Media

BA (Hons) Computer Animation
University of Teeside

BA (Hons) Computer Visualisation and Animation
Bournemouth Media School

BA (Hons) Design Animation
North East Wales Institute of Higher Education

BA (Hons) Design: Animation
Staffordshire University

BA (Hons) Design for Interactive Media with digital animation
London College of Music and Media

BA (Hons) Film and Animation Production
The Arts Institute at Bournemouth

BA (Hons) Graphic Arts Animation
Liverpool John Moores University

BA (Hons) Graphic Design (Animation)
Norwich School of Graphic Art and Design

BA (Hons) Media Production with Animation
University of Luton

BA (Hons) Multimedia Design and Digital Animation
Cumbria College of Art and Design

BA (Hons) Photography and Digital Imaging with Digital Animation
London College of Music and Media

BA (Hons) Visual Communication (Animation)
Edinburgh College of Art

BDes (Hons) Animation and Electronic Media
Duncan of Jordanstone College of Art and Design

BSc Computer Animation and Special Effects
University of Bradford

BSc (Foundation Degree) Computer Visualisation and Animation
Ravensbourne College of Design and Communication

BSc (Hons) Multimedia Computing with Digital Animation
London College of Music and Media

HNC in 3D Computer Animation
James Watt College

HNC in Filmcraft and Animation
Motherwell College

HND in 3D Computer Animation
James Watt College

HND in Animation
Glamorgan Centre for Art and Design Technology

HND in Animation and Creative Media
Plymouth College of Art and Design

HND in Animation Production
James Watt College

HND in Design Technology (Multimedia, Broadcast Graphics and Animation)
Farnborough College of Technology

HND in Filmcraft and Animation
Motherwell College

LOCN Animation and Multimedia
Tower Hamlets College

MA in Animation
North East Wales Institute of Higher Education
Royal College of Art

MA in Film and Television (Animation Direction)
National Film and Television School

Mphil and PhD in Animation
Royal College of Art

National Diploma in Media and Animation with Model making for Film and Television
Bridgewater College

WNYOCN Animation Workshop – Level 3
York College

BUSINESS

BA (Hons) Advertising with Business
London College of Music and Media

BA (Hons) Business Economics and Film Studies (Modular)
Bolton Institute of Higher Education

BA (Hons) Business Information Systems and Film Studies (Modular)
Bolton Institute of Higher Education

BA (Hons) Business Studies and Film Studies
Bolton Institute of Higher Education

BA (Hons) Communicatioon Studies (EFL) and Business
Buckingham University

HND in Business (Arts and Media Management)
New College Durham

CAMERA

Camera Operations – Max Q
Line Out

NVQ Camera (Level 2)
Grimsby College 35

NVQ Camera (Level 3)
Grimsby College

CINEMATOGRAPHY

MA in Film and Television (Cinematography – Film and Video)
National Film and Television School

COMPOSING

Bmus (Hons) Performance and Composition
London College of Music and Media

Composing and Synchronising Music to Film and Video
Westminster Adult Education Service

MA in Composing for Film and Television
Kingston University

Mmus in Composing for Film and Television
London College of Music and Media

DIRECTING

Directing Actors for Camera
North Kensington Video-Drama Project

Directing Diploma
ARTS International

Documentary Production and Direction
North Kensington Video – Drama Project

MA in Film and Television (Animation Direction)
National Film and Television School

MA in Film and Television (Documentary Direction)
National Film and Television School

MA in Film and Television (Fiction Direction)
National Film and Television School

ECONOMICS

BA (Hons) Business Economics and Film Studies (Modular)
Bolton Institute of Higher Education

BA (Hons) Media and Popular Culture with Economics
University College, Northampton

EDITING
BA (Hons) Editorial and Advertising Photography

Kent Institute of Art and Design

Editing – Non-linear and Linear – Max Q
Line Out

HNC in Broadcast Post production
Ravensbourne College of Design and Communication

MA in Film and Television Editing
National Film and Television School

NVQ Edit (Level 2)
Grimsby College

NVQ Edit (Level 3)
Grimsby College

PgCert and PgDip in Script Editing
Liverpool John Moores University

HAIRDRESSING

Film and Television Make-Up, Hair Design, Wigmaking and Special Effects Course
Retford International College

Historic Hairdressing NVQ Level 3 (Long Hair, Wig and Hairpiece Design Attachment)
Retford International College

Make-Up and Hairdressing – Toatl Look Fashion
Retford International College

The Complete Make-up Artist Training programme
Delamar Academy of Makeup

MAKE-UP
Certificate of Higher Education in Professional Make-Up Design

Delamar Academy of Make-up

Edexcel Professional Development Certificate in Media Make-Up
Westminster Adult Education Service

Film and Television Make-Up, Hair Design, Wigmaking and Special Effects Course
Retford International College

HND in Theatrical and Media Make-Up
Somerset College of Arts and Technology

Make-Up and Hairdressing – Total Look Fashion
Retford International College

Make-Up Artists Diploma
North-east Worcestershire College

National Diploma in Media Make-Up
Stockport College in Further and Higher Education

Speciality make-Up
Retford International College

Television, Film and Video Make-Up
Retford International College

The Complete Make-Up Artist Training programme
Delamar Academy of make-Up

Theatrical make-Up (Character)
Retford International College

Total Look – Advanced
Retford International College

Total Look make-Up
Retford International College

Total Look make-Up (Character)
Retford International College

MARKETING

BA (Hons) Advertising with marketing
London College of Music and Media

BA (Hons) Film Studies and Marketing (Modular)
Bolton Institute of Higher Education

BA (Hons) Media and Marketing
Farnborough College of Technology

BA (Hons) Media and Popular Culture with marketing Communications
University College Northampton

BSc in Marketing with Media Communications
University of Buckingham

HNC in Marketing
Central College of Commerce

HND in Business (Advertising and Marketing Communications)
West Herts College

HND in marketing
Central College of Commerce

Scottish Group Award in Communication and Media (Higher) Marketing
Glasgow College of Building and Printing

POST PRODUCTION

HNC in Broadcast Post-Production
Ravensbourne College of Design and Communication

PRODUCING

MA in Film and Television (Producing)
National Film and Television School

MA in Producing Film and Television
Royal Holloway

SCREENWRITING

BA (Hons) Screenwriting (Media Practice Programme)
Central Lancashire University

MA in Feature Film Screenwriting
Royal Holloway

MA in Film and Television Screenwriting
National Film and Television School

MA in Screenwriting
London College of Printing

MA in Screenwriting (Fiction)
Leeds Metropolitan University
Northern Film School

PgCert PgDip and MA in Screen writing
Liverpool John Moores University

Screenwriting
North Kensington Video-Drama Project

SCRIPTWRITING

BA (Hons) Media Performance with Scriptwriting
University of Luton

BA (Hons) Scriptwriting for Film and Television
Bournemouth Media School

MA in Television Scriptwriting
De Montfort University Leicester

PgDip and MA in Television and Radio Scriptwriting
University of Salford

PgDip in Dramatic Writing
University of Sussex

Scriptwiring
Hulme Adult learning Centre

SET DESIGN

BA (Hons) Technical Arts: Design
Wimbledon School of Arts

Setcrafts Apprenticeship Training Scheme
FT2-Film and Television Freelance Training

SOUND

Audion – Max Q
Line Out

BA (Hons) Another Subject with Sound and Music Recording
London College of Music and Media

BA (Hons) Digital Arts with Sound and Music Recording
London College of Music and Media

BSc (Hons) Audio Technology
University of Salford
Southampton Institute

BSc (Hons) Creative Music and Sound Technology
Leeds Metropolitan University

Certificates, Diplomas and Degrees in Audio and Multimedia
S and E Technology College

Foundation Sound and Vision
East Surrey College

HND in Professional Sound and Video Technology
University of Salford

MA in Film and Television (Screen Sound)
National Film and Television School

MA in Sound Design for the Moving Image
Bournemouth Media School

National Certificate in Sound Recording and Media production
North Glasgow College

National Diploma in Media (Audio and Moving Image)
North West Institute of Further and Higher Education

National Diploma in Media Production (Audio)
Lewisham College

National Diploma in Media Production (Audio and Moving Image)
Cambridge Regional College

Darlington College of Technology
Oxford College of Further Education

Sound Engineering Studies
Perth College

(2) Further Education Colleges and Universities offering a wide variety of film-related subjects – all colleges in section one are listed in alphabetical order

ABERDEEN COLLEGE, Gallowgate, Aberdeen, Scotland AB25 1BN
www.abcol.ac.uk 01224 612023

AABBINGDON COLLEGE, Northcourt Road, Abingdon, Oxford OX14 1NN 01235 555585 Email mgaston@abingdoncollege.ac.uk

ACCRINGTON AND ROSSENDALE COLLEGE, Division of Academic and Lifelong Learning, Sandy Lane, Accrington, Lancashire BB5 2AW. 01254 354219

AFECT
(Advancement of Film Education Charitable Trust), 52a Waltham Grove, London SW6 1QR
020 7609 2992

AMERSHAM AND WYCOMBE COLLEGE Stanley Hill, Amersham
Bucks HP7 9HN
www.amersham.ac.uk 01494 735555

ANGUS COLLEGE, Keptie Road, Arbroath, Angus, DD1 3EA. www.angus.ac.uk
01241 432600

THE ARTS INSTITUTE AT BOURNEMOUTH, School of Media, Wallisdown, Poole, Dorset BH12 5HH. www.arts-inst boutnemouth.ac.uk. 01202 363320

ARRTS INTERNATIONAL, Highfield Grange, Bubwith, North Yorks YO8 6DP. www.arrts.co.uk. 01757 288088.

AYR COLLEGE, Dam Park, Ayr, South Ayrshire KA8 OEU. 0800 199798

BARKING COLLEGE, Dagenham Road, Romford, Essex RM7 PXU
www.barking-coll.ac.uk 01708 770000

BARNET COLLEGE, Wood Street, High Barnet, Herts EN5 4AZ
www.barnet.ac.uk 020 8440 6321

BARNFIELD College, New Bedford Road, Luton, Beds LU2 7BF. 01582 569 627.

BARNSLEY COLLEGE, Honeywell Site, Honeywell Lane, Barnsley, South Yorkshire,
S75 1BP. www.barnsley.ac.uk 01226 216216.

BARNSLEY COLLEGE, New Electric Theatre Studios, PO Box 266, Church Street,
Barnsley, South Yorkshire, S70 2YW. www.barnsley.ac.uk 01226 216129

BARNSLEY COLLEGE, Old Mill lane Site, Church Street, Barnsley, S70 2AX.
www.barnsley.ac.uk. 01226 730191.

BASINGSTOKE COLLEGE OF TECHNOLOGY, School Of Design and
Communications, Worting Road, Basingstoke, Hampshire, RG21 1TN. 010256 306228.

UNIVERSITY OF BATH, Claverton Down, Bath, BA2 7AY. www.bath.ac.uk. 01225
323491.

BEDFORD COLLEGE OF HIGHER EDUCATION, Cauldwell Street, Bedford,
MK42 9AH. www.bedford.ac.uk. 01234 291525

BELFAST INSTITUTE FOR FURTHER AND HIGHER EDUCATION, Ormeau
Avenue, Ravenhil Road, Belfast, BT6 4GZ. 028 9026 537.

BELL COLLEGE, Almada Street, Hamilton, Lanarkshire ML3 OJB. www.bell.ac.uk.
01698 283100

BEVERLEY COLLEGE, Gallows Lane, Beverley, East Yorkshire, HU17 7DT.
www.beverleycollege.ac.uk 01482 868362.

BEXLEY COLLEGE, St Josephs Campus, 269 Woolwich Road, Abbeywood, London SE2 OAR. www.bexley.ac.uk. 01322 404277.

BLACBURN COLLEGE, The Media Centre, Fielden Street, Blackburn Lancashire, BB2 1LH. 01254 292167.

BLACKPOOL AND THE FYLDE COLLEGE, Ashfield Road, Bispham, Blackpool FY2 OHB. www.blackpool.ac.uk. 01253 352352.

BLACKPOOL AND THE FYLD COLLEGE, Central Blackpool Campus, Palatine Road, Blackpool, Lancs FY1 4DW www.blackpool.ac.uk. 01253 352352.

BLAKE COLEGE, 162 New Cavendish Street, London W1M 7FJ. www.blake.ac.uk. 020 7636 0658.

BOLTON COLLEGE, Manchester Road, Bolton, BL2 1ER. www.bolton-college.ac.uk. 01204 531411.

BOLTON INSTITUTE OF HIGHER EDUCATION Chadwick Campus, Chadwick Street, Bolton BL2 1JW www.asc.bolton.ac.uk/human/film/filmhome.htm 01204 528851

BORDERS COLEGE, Thorniedean, Melrose Road, Galashiels, TD1 2AF. www.borderscollege.ac.uk. 01896 756440.

BOURNEMOUTH MEDIA SCOOL, Bournemouth University, Talbot Campus, Fern Barrow, Poole Dorset BH12 5BB. Media.Bournemouth.ac.uk 01202 595745.

BRADFORD UNIVERSITY, Department of Electronic Imaging and Media Communication, Bradford, West Yorkshire BD7 1DP www.eimc.brad.ac.uk 01274 235748

BRIDGEWATER COLLEGE, Bath Road, Bridgewater, Somerset, TA6 4PZ. 01278 455464.

BRIGHTON COLLEGE OF TECHNOLOGY, Pelham Street, Brighton, BN1 4FA. www.bricoltech.ac.uk. 01273 667788.

BRITISH ANIMATION TRAING SCHEME, Museum of the Moving Image, South Bank, Waterloo, London SE1 8XT. 020 7815 1346.

BROOKLANDS COLLEGE, Media Section, Heath Road, Weybridge, Surrey, KT13 8TT. www.brooklands.ac.uk. 01932 797726.

UNVERSITY OF BUCKINGHAM, School of Languages Hunter Street, Buckingham, MK18 1EG www.buckingham.ac.uk 01280 814080

BURNLEY COLLEGE, Ormerod Road, Burnley, Lancs BB11 2RX. 01282 436111.
CALDERDALE COLLEGE, Halifax School of Integrated Arts, Francis Street, Halifax, HX1 3UZ. 01422 399399.

CAMBRIDGE ARTS AND SCIENCES, School of Arts and Design, 13-14 Round Church Road, Cambridge, CB5 8AD. www.ccg-uk-com. 01223 314431.

CAMBRIDGE REGIONAL COLLEGE, Kings Hedges Road, Cambridge, CB4 2QT. www.camrc.ac.uk. 01223 418200.

UNIVERSITY OF CAMBRIDGE, Board of Continuing Education, Madingley Hall, Madingley, Cambridge, CB3 8AQ. www.cont-ed.cam.ac.uk. 01954 280226.

CANTERBURY CHRIST CHURCH UNIVERSITY COLLEGE, Canterbury, Kent, CT1 1QU. www.cant.ac.uk. 01277 767700.

CANTERBURY COLLEGE, New Dover Road, Canterbury, Kent CT1 3AJ. www.cant-col.ac.uk. 01277 811341.

CARDONALD COLLEGE, 690 Mosspark Drive, Cardonlad, Glasgow, G52 3AY. www.cardonald.ac.uk. 0141 272 3242.

CARMARTHENSHIRE COLLEGE, Graig Campus, Sandy Road, Llanelli, SA15 4DN. www.ccta.ac.uk. 01554 748000.

CARSHALTON COLLEGE, Media, Arts and Design Centre, Nightingale Road, Carshalton, Surrey, SM5 2EJ. www.carshalton.ac.uk. 020 87706825.

CAUSEWAY INSTITUTE OF FURTHER AND HIGHER EDUCATION, 2 Colerain Road, Ballymoney, County Antrim, Northern Ireland, BT52 6BP. www.causeway.ac.uk. 028 2766 0419.

CENTRAL COLLEGE OF COMMERCE, 300 Cathedral Street, Glasgow, G1 2TA. 0141 52 3941.

CENTRAL LANCASHIRE UNIVERSITY, Faculty of Design and Technology, Department of Art and fashion, Victoria Building, Preston Lancashire PR1 2HE www.uclan.ac.uk 01772 893199

CHELMSFORD COLLEGE, Moulsham Street, Chelmsford, CM2 OJO. 01242 543236.

CHICHESTER COLLEGE OF ARTS SCIENCE AND TECHNOLOGY, Westgate Fields, Chichester, West Sussex, PO19 1SB. www.chichester.ac.uk. 01243 786321.

CIRENCESTER COLLEGE, Stroud Road, Cirencester, Glos GL7 1XA. 01285 640994.

CITY AND ISLINGTON COLLEGE, Islington Campus, 444 Camden Road, London N7 0SP. www.candi.ac.uk. 020 7700 8600.

CITY COLLEGE MANCHESTER, Arden Centre, Northenden, Manchester, M23 ODD. www.multimedia.ccm.ac.uk.

CITY COLLEGE MANCHESTER, Sale road, Northenden, Manchester, M23 ODD. www.ccm.ac.uk. 0161 957 1749.

CITY COLLEGE NORWICH, Ipswich Road, Norwich, NR2 2LJ. www.ccn.ac.uk. 01603 773269.

CITY OF BRISTOL COLLEGE, Ashley Down Road, Ashley Down, Bristol, BS7 9BU. www.cityofbristol.ac.uk. 0177 904 5143.

CITY OF WESTMINSTER COLLEGE, 25 Paddington Green, London W2 1NB. 020 7258 2789.

CLARENDON CITY COLLEGE, New College, Nottingham, The Adams Building, Stoney Street, Lace Market, Nottingham, NG1 1NG. www.cnc.ac.uk. 0115 910 4665.

CLEVELAND COLLEGE OF ART AND DESIGN, Green Lane, Linthorpe, Middlesborough, TS5 7RJ. www.ccad.ac.uk. 01642 288000.

CLYDEBANK COLLEGE, Kilbowie Road, Clydebank G81 2AA. www.clydebankcoollege.ac.uk. 0141 952 7771.

COATBRIDGE COLEGE, Kildoman Street, Coatbridge, Lanarkshire ML5 3LS. 01236 422316.

COLCHESTER INSTITUTE, Sheepen Road, Colchester, CO3 3LL. 01206 518144.

COLEG GLAN HAFREN, Trowbridge Road, Rumney, Cardiff, CF3 1XZ. www.glan-hafren-ac-uk. 029 2025 0319.

COLEG MENAI, Bangor, Gwynedd LL55 2TP. 01248 370125.

CORNWALL COLLEGE, Pool, Redruth,Cornwall, TR15 3RD. www.cornwall.ac.uk. 01209 611611.

CRAVEN COLLEGE, High Street, Skipton, North Yorkshire, BD23 1JY. 01756 791411.

CRAWLEY COLLEGE, College Road, Crawley, West Sussex, RH10 1NR. 01293 442311.

CRICKLADE COLLEGE, Charlton Road, Andover, Hampshire, SP10 1EJ. www.cricklade.ac.uk. 01264 334222.

CUMBRIA COLLEGE OF ART AND DESIGN, Brampton Road, Carlisle, Cumbria, CA3 9AY. www.cumbriacad.ac.uk. 01228 400300.

CYFLE CYF, Gronant, Penrallt Isaf, Gwynedd, LL5 1NW. www.cyfle.co.uk. 01286 671000.

CYFLE CYF, Ty Critchon, 11-12 Mount Street Square, Caerdydd CF1 6EE. www.cyfle.co.uk. 029 2046 5533..

DARLINGTON COLLEGE OF TECHNOLOGY, Cleveland Avenue, Darlington, co. Durham DL3 7BB. 01325 503229

DELEMAR ACADEMY OF MAKE-UP, 52A Waltham Grove. Fulham, London, SW6 1QR. www.themake-upcentre.co.uk 020 7381 0213.

DE MONTFORT UNIVERSITY LEICESTER , Faculty of Art and Design, The Gateway, Leicester LE1 9BH. www.dmu.ac.uk 0116 257 7507

DUDLEY COLLEGE, Mons Hill Site, 11 Wrens Hill Road, Dudley, West Midlands DY1 3SB. 01384 363192.

DUMFRIES AND GALLOWAY, Dumfries and Galloway, DG1 3QZ. www.dumgal.ac.uk 01387 243893

DUNCAN OF JORDANSTONE College of Art and Design, University of Dundee, School of Television and Imaging, perth Road, Dundee DD1 4HT www.imaging.dundee.ac.uk 01382 345250

DUNDEE COLLEGE, Media Section, 30 Constitution Road Centre, Dundee, DD3 6TB. 01382 834834.

DUNSTABLE COLLEGE, Kingsway, Dunstable, LU5 4HG. 01582 477776.

EAST ANTRIM INSTITUTE OF FURTHER EDUCATION, 400 Shore Road, Newtownabbey, County Antrim Northern Ireland BT37 9RS. 028 9086 4331.

EAST DURHAM AND HOUGHALL COMMUNITY COLLEGE, Peterlee, Co. Durham SR8 1NU. 0191 518 2000.

EAST SURREY COLLEGE, Media Division, Gatton Point North, Claremont Road, Redhill, Surrey, RH1 2JX. www.esc.org.uk. 01737 772611.

EASTBOURNE COLLEGE OF ARTS AND TECHNOLOGY, ECAT House, Cross Levels Way, Eastbourne, BN21 2UF. 01323 644711.

EDINGBURGH COLLEGE OF ART School of Visual Communication, 74 Lauriston Place, Edinburgh, EH3 9DF. www.eca.ac.uk 0131 221 6138

EDINBURGH VIDEO TRAINING COMPANY LIMITED Unit 22, John Cotton Centre, 10 Sunnyside, Edinburgh, EH7 5RA. 0131 652 1206.

EPPING FOREST COLLEGE, Borders lane, Loughton, Essex, 1G10 3SA. 020 8508 8311.

FAREHAM COLLEGE, Bishopsfield Road, Fareham, Hampshire, PO14 1NH. www.farcham.ac.uk. 01329 815346.

FARNBOROUGH COLLEGE OF TECHNOLOGY, School of Media and Visual Arts, Boundary Road, Farnborough, Hampshire GU14 6SB. www.farn-ct.ac.uk. 01252 407 270.

FIRST FILM FOUNDATION, 9 Bourlet Close, London W1P 7PJ www.firstfilm.co.uk. 020 7580 2111.

Ft2-FILM AND TELEVISION FEELANCE TRAINING, Fourth Floor, Warwick House, 9 Warwick Street, LONDON W1R 5RA. www.ft2.org.uk 020 7734 5141.

GLAMORGAN CENTRE FOR ART AND DESIGN, Glyntaff Road, Glyntaff, Pontypridd, Mid Glamorgan CF37 4AT. 01443 663309

GLASGOW COLLEGE OF BUILDING AND PRINTING, 60 North Hanover Street, Glasgow, G1 2BP. www.gchp.ac.uk o141 332 969.

GRIMSBY COLLEGE, Nuns Corner, Grimsby NE Lincolnshire DN34 5BQ. www.grimsby.ac.uk. 01472 311222.

GUILDFORD COLLEGE, Stoke Park, Guildford, Surrey, GU1 1EZ. 01483 448500.

HACKNEY COMMUNITY COLLEGE, Shoreditch Campus, Falkirk Street, London N1 6HQ. www.comm-coll-hackney.ac.uk. 020 7613 9123.

HAMMERSMITH AND WEST LONDON COLLEGE, Gliddon Road, Barons Court, London W14 9BL. www.hwlc.ac.uk. 020 8741 1688.

HARLOW COLLEGE, Velizey Avenue, Harlow, Essex. CM20 3LH. www.harlow-college.ac.uk 01279 868000

HAVERING COLLEGE OF FURTHER AND HIGHER EDUCATION, Havering Acadmey of Arts and Sciences, Ardleigh Green Road, Hornchurch, Essex

RM11 2LL. www.havering-college.ac.uk 01708 455011.

HENLEY COLLEGE, COVENTRY, Department of Hospitality and Creative Studies, Henley Road, Bell Green, Coventry CV2 1ED. www.henley-cov.ac.uk. 024 7667 6300.

THE HENLEY COLLEGE, Deanfield Avenue, Henley, Oxon, RG9 1UH. www.henleycol.ac.uk. 01491 579988.

HOXTON HALL, 130 Hoxton Street, London N1 6SH. www.hoxtonhall.dobsol.co.uk 020 7684 0060.

HULL COLLEGE, Riley Centre, Parkefield Drive, Hull, HU3 6TE. www.hull college.ac.uk 01482 351228.

HULME ADULT LEARNING CENTRE, Hulme Centre, Stretford Road, Manchester M15 5FQ. 0161 226 8411.

HULME ADULT LEARNING CENTRE, Hulme Walk, Hulme, Manchester M15 5FQ. . 0161 226 8411.

INTERMEDIA FILM AND VIDEO (NOTTINGHAM) Ltd, 19 Heathcote Street, Nottingham NG1 3AF, www.intermedianotts.co.uk. 0115 955 6909.

INVERNESS COLLEGE, 3 Longman Road, Longman South, Inverness 1V1 1SA. 01463 273353.

JAMES WATT COLLEGE, Finnart Street, Greenock, Renfrewshire, PA16 8HF. www.jameswatt.ac.uk 01475 724433.

JAMES WATT COLLEGE, North Ayrshire Campus, Lauchlan way, Kilwinning, North Ayrshire www.jameswatt.ac.uk 01294 555314.

KENT INSTITUTE OF ART AND DESIGN, Maidstone College, Oakwood Park, Maidstone, Kent ME16 8AG. 01622 757286

KINGSTON COLLEGE, Division of Media and Performing Arts, Department of Design Studies, Kingston Hall Road, Kingston Upon Thames, Surrey KT1 2AQ. 020 8 268 2897.

LAMBETH COLLEGE, Vauxhall centre, Belmore Street, Wandsworth Road, London SW8 2JY. www.lambethcollege.ac.uk 020 7501 5618.

LEEDS COLLEGE OF ARTS AND DESIGN, Jacob Kramer Buildings, Blenheim walk, Leeds, LS2 9AQ. www.leeds-art.ac.uk 0113 202 8136.

LEEDS COLLEGE OF MUSIC, 3 Quarry Hill, Leeds, LS2 7PD. www.lcm.ac.uk 0113 222 3400.

LEEDS METROLPOLITAN UNIVERSITY, Calverley Street, Leeds, LS1 3HE. www.lmu.ac.uk 0113 283 3113.

LEICESTER COLLEGE, St Margaret's Campus, Grafton Place, St John Street, Leicester, LE1 3WL. www.leicestercollege.ac.uk 0116 224 2002.

LEWISHAM COLLEGE, Tressilian Building, Lewisham Way, London SE4 1UT. www.lewisham.ac-uk/college 020 8692 0353.

LIGHT HOUSE, The Chubb Building, Fryer Street, Wolverhampton, WV1 1HT. www.light-house.co.uk 01902 716055

LIGHTHOUSE, 9-12 Middle Street, Brighton, BN1 1AL. www.lighthouse.org.uk 01273 384258.

LINE OUT, Fosse Arts Centre, Mantle Road, Leicester, LE3 5HG. 0116 262 1265.

LIVERPOOL COMMUNITY COLLEGE, Professional media, The Arts Centre, 9 Myrtle Street, Liverpool, L7 7JA. www.liv-coll.ac.uk 0151 252 4328

LIVERPOOL JOHN MOORES UNIVERSITY, School of Media, Critical and Creative Arts, Dean Walters Building, St James Road, Liverpool L1 7BR www.livjm.ac.uk 0151 231 5052

LONDON COLLEGE OF MUSIC AND MEDIA, Thames Valley University, St Mary's Road, Ealing, London W5 5RF elgar.tvu.ac.uk 020 8231 2022

LONDON FILM MAKING ACADEMY, The Old Church, 52a Waltham Grove, London SW6 1QR. www.londonfilmacademy.com 020 7386 7711.

LOUGHBOROUGH COLLEGE, Community and General Education, Radmore road, Loughborough, Leicestershire, LE11 3BT. www.loucoll.ed.uk 01509 215831.

MERTON COLLEGE, Central Road, Mordern, Surrey SM4 5SE. www.merton.ac.uk 020 8408 8663.

MORLEY COLLEGE, 61 Westminster Bridge Road, London SE1 7HT. www.morleycollege.ac.uk 020 7450 9235.

MOTHERWEL COLLEGE, Dalzell Drive, Motherwell, ML1 2DD. www.motherwell.ac.uk. 01698 232652.

NATIONAL FILM AND TELEVISION SCHOOL, Beaconsfield Studios, Station Road, Beaconsfiled, Bucks, HP9 1LG www.nftsfilm-tv.ac.uk 01494 671234

NERVE CENTRE, 7-8 Magazine Street, Derry City, Northern Ireland, BT48 6HJ. www.nerve-centre.org.uk 028 7126 0562.

NESCOT (NORTH EAST SURREY COLLEGE OF TECHNOLOGY), Reigate Road, Ewell, Surrey, KT17 3DS. www.nescot.ac.uk. 020 8394 3192.

NEW COLLEGE DURHAM, Nevilles cross Centre, Darlington Road, Durham, DH1 4SY www.newdur.ac.uk 0191 375 4118

NEW COLLEGE SWINDON, Helston Road, Park North, Swindon, SN3 2LA. 01793 611470.

NEW PRODUCERS ALLIANCE, 9 Bourlet Close, London W1W 7BP. www.newproducer.co.uk 020 7580 2480.

NEWBURY COLLEGE OF FURTHER EDUCATION, Oxford Road, Newbury Berks RG13 1PQ. 01635 37000.

NEWCASTLE COLLEGE, School of Arts and Design, John marley Centre, Wickham View, Newcastle Upon Tyne NE15 6T. www.ncl-coll.ac.uk 0191 200 4725.

NEWCASTLE COLLEGE, School of Music and Performing Arts, Rye Hill Campus, Scotswood Road, Newcastle upon Tyne, NE4 7SA. www.ncl-coll.ac.uk 0191 200 4684.

NEWCASTLE UNDER LYME COLLEGE, Liverpool Road, Newcastle Under Lyme, Staffordshire, ST5 2DF. 10782 254325.

NORTHBOROOK COLLEGE, Litlehampton Road, Goring by Sea, Worthing, West Sussex BN12 6NU www.northbrok.ac.uk 01903 606001

NORTH EAST WALES INSTITUTE OF HIGHER EDUCATION, North wales School of Art and Design, 49 Regent Street, Wrexham, LL11 1PF. www.newi.ac.uk/nwsad 01978 293552.

NORTH EAST WORCESTERSHIRE COLLEGE, Redditch Campus, Peakman Street, Redditch, Worcs B98 8DW. 01527 570020

NORTH WEST INSTITUTE OF FURTHER AND HIGHER EDUCATION, Strand Road, Londonderry BT48 7BY www.nwifhe.ac.uk 028 7126 6711

NORTH GLASGOW COLLEGE, 110 Flemington Street, Glasgow, G21 4BX. www.north-gla.ac.uk. 0141 558 9001.

NORTH HERTFORDSHIRE COLLEGE, Stevenage Centre, Monkswood way, Stevenage, Herts, SG1 1LA. 01462 424242.

NORTH KENSINGTON VIDEO DRAM PROJECT, 1 Thorpe Close, London W10 5XL. 020 8964 2641.

NORTH NOTTINGHAMSHIRE COLLEGE, Carlton Road, Worksop, Notts S81 7HP. 01909 473561.

NORTH OXFORDSHIRE COLLEGE, Broughton Road, Banbury, Oxon, OX16 9QA. www.northox.ac.uk 01295 252221.

NORTHERN FILM SCHOOL Leeds Metropolitan University, 2 Queens Square, Leeds LS2 8AF. www. lmu.ac.uk/hen/aad/nfs 0113 283 1900

NORTH WARWICKSHIRE AND HINCKLEY COLLEGE, New Media and Performing Arts Centre, London Road, Hinckley, Leicestershire LE10 1HQ. www.nwarks-hinckley.ac.uk. 024 7634 9321.

NORWICH SCHOOL OF GRAPHIC ART AND DESIGN, St George Street, Norwich NR3 1BB www.nsad.ac.uk 01603 610561

OAKLANDS COLLEGE, Art, Media and Performing Arts, St Albans City Campus, St Peters Road, St Albans, Herts, AL1 3RX. 01707 737000.

THE OLDHAM COLLEGE, School of Visual and performing Arts, Rochdale Road, Oldham, OL9 6AA. www.oldham.ac.uk. 0161 785 4052.

OXFORD COLEGE OF FURTHER EDUCATION, Faculty of Arts, Oxpens Road, Oxford, OX1 1SA. www.oxfe.ac.uk/ocfe 01865 269482.

PEMBROKESHIRE COLLEGE, Merlins Bridge, Haverfordwest, Pembrokeshire, SA61 1SZ. www.pembrokeshire.ac.uk 01437 765247.

THE PEOPLE COLLEGE NOTTINGHAM, Maid Marian Way, Nottingham, NG1 6AB. www.peoples.ac.uk 0115 912 3500.

PERTH COLLEGE, Faculty of Arts, Goodyburn East, Crieff Road, Perth, Perthshire PH1 2NX. www.uhi.ac.uk/perth 01738 621171.

PLYMOUTH COLLEGE OF ART AND DESIGN, Tavistock Place, Plymouth, PL4 8AT. www.pcad.plym.ac.uk 01752 203434.

PONTYPRIDD COLLEGE, YNYS Terrace, Rhydyfelin, Pontypridd, Mid Glamorgan CF37 5RN. www.pontypridd.ac.uk. 01443 663090.

QUEEN ELIZABETH'S FOUNDATION TRAINING COLLEGE, Leatherhead Court, Leatherhead, KT22 OBN. 01372 841100.

RAVENSBOURNE COLEGE OF DESIGN AND COMMUNICATION, Walden Road, Chislehurst, Kent BR7 5SN www.rave.ac.uk 020 8289 4900

REDBRIDGE COLLEGE, Little Heath, Romford, Essex, RM6 4XT. 020 8548 7400.

RETFORD INTERNATIONAL COLLEGE, 11 Grove Street, Retford, Notts, DN22 6PJ. (Make up and design) 01777707371.

RICHMOND UPON THAMES COLLEGE, Media Education Workshop, Egerton Road, Twickenham, TW2 7SJ. 020 8607 8217.

ROYAL COLLEGE OF TECHNOLOGY, Kensington Gore, London SW7 2EU www.rca.ac.uk 020 7590 4512

ROYAL HOLLWAY, University of London, Department of Media Arts Egham Surrey TW20 OEX www.media.dr.rhul.ac.uk 01784 443734

ST AUSTELL COLLEGE, Trevarthian Road, St Austell, Cornwall, PL25 4BU. 01726 67911.

ST HELENS COLLEGE, School of Arts, Media and Design, Town Centre Campus, Brook Street, St Helens, Merseyside, WA10 1PZ. www.sthelens.ac.uk. 01744 623253.

ST VINCENT COLLEGE, Mill Lane, Gosport, Hants PO12 4QA. 023 9258 8311.

UNIVERSITY OF SALFORD, Salford M5 4WT. www.salford.ac.uk 0161 295 5321.

SANDWELL COLLEGE, Lakeside Studios, Smethwick Campus, Crocketts Lane, Smethwick, West Midlands B66 3BU. www.sandwell.ac.uk 0121 253 6341.

SELBY COLLEGE, Department of Art, Design and Media, Abbots Road, Selby YO8 8AT. www.selbycollege.co.uk. 01757 211000.

THE SHEFFIELD COLLEGE, Norton Centre, Dyche Lane, Sheffiled S8 8BR. www.sheffcol.ac.uk 0114 260 2300.

SIF (Sheffield Independent Film), 5 Brown Street, Sheffield, S1 2BS. 0114 272 0304.

SOMERSET COLLEGE OF ARTS AND TECHNOLOGY, Wellington Road, Taunton, Somerset TA1 5AX. www.somerset.ac.uk 01823 366311.

SOUTHAMPTON INSTITUTE, East Park Terrace, Southampton, SO14 OYN www.solent.ac.uk

SOUTH CHESHIRE COLLEGE, Creative and Performing Arts, Dane Bank Avenue, Crewe, Cheshire, CW2 8AB. www.s-cheshire.ac.uk 01270 654654.

SOUTH DEVON COLLEGE, Newton Road, Torre, Torquay, Devon,TQ2 5BY. 01803 406253

SOUTH DOWNS COLLEGE OF FURTHER EDUCATION, College Road, Havant, Hampshire, PO7 8AA. 023 9279 7979.

SOUTH EAST ESSEX COLLEGE, Carnarvon Road, Southend on Sea, Essex SS2 6LS. www.se-essex-college.ac.uk. 01702 220400.

SOUTH KENT COLLEGE, The Media Centre, Maison Dieu Road, Dover, Kent, CT16 1DH. 01304 244355.

SOUTH THAMES COLLEGE, Faculty of Creative and Technological Studies, Wandsworth High Street, London SW18 2PP. www.south-thames.ac.uk 020 8918 7315.

SOUTH TRAFFORD COLLEGE, Manchester Road, Timperley, Cheshire, WA14 5PQ. 0161 952 4733.

SOUTHGATE COLLEGE, High Street, London N14 6BS. www.southgate.ac.uk 020 8982 5064.

SOUTHWARK COLLEGE, Surrey Docks Centre, Drummond Road, London SE16 4EE. www.southwark.ac.uk. 020 7815 1500.

STEVENSON COLLEGE, Bankhead Avenue, Sighthill, Edinburgh, EH1 4DE. www.stevenson.ac.uk 0131 535 4600.

STOCKPORT COLLEGE OF FURTHER AND HIGHER EDUCATION, Wellington Road South, Stockport, Cheshire SK1 3UQ. www.stockport.ac.uk 0161 958 3168.

STRATFORD UPON AVON COLLEGE, The Willows North, Stratford Upon Avon Warwickshire CV37 9QR. 01789 266254.

STROUD COLLEGE OF FURTHER EDUCATION, Stratford Road, Stroud, Glos, GL5 4AH. 01453 763424.

SURREY INSTITUE OF ART AND DESIGN, Falkner Road, The Hart, Farnham, Surrey GU9 7DS www.surrart.ac.uk 01252 722441

SUTTON COLDFIELD COLEGE OF FURTHER EDUCATION, Lichfield Road, Sutton Coldfield, Birmingham, B74 2NW. www.sutcol.ac.uk 0121 355 5671.

SWANSEA COLLEGE, Tychoch Road, Swansea, SA2 9EB. www.swancoll.ac.uk. 01792 284023.

SWINDON COLLEGE, School of Art and Design, Euclid Street, Swindon, Wiltshire, SN21 2JQ. www.swindon-college.ac.uk. 01793 498490.

TAMESIDE COLLEGE, Clarendon Road, Hyde, Cheshire, SK14 2JZ. www.tamesidecollege.ac.uk 0161 908 6800.

TEESIDE TERTIARY COLLEGE, Faculty of Creative Arts and Media, Longlands Campus, Douglas Street, Middlesborough, Cleveland TS4 2JW. www.ttc.ac.uk 01642 275000.

TELFORD COLLEGE OF ARTS AND TECHNOLOGY, Haybridge Road, Wellington, Telford, Shropshire TF1 2NP. www.tcat.ac.uk 01952 642211.

THOMAS DANBY COLLEGE, Rounday Road, Leeds LS7 3BG. www.thomasdanby.ac.uk. 0113 284 6220.

TOTTON COLLEGE, Water Lane, Totton, Southampton SO40 3ZX. www.totton.ac.uk. 023 8087 4874.

TOWER HAMLETS COLLEGE, Poplar Centre, Poplar High Street, London E14 OAF. www.tower.ac.uk 020 7538 5888.

TRESHAM INSTITUTE OF FURTHER AND HIGHER EDUCATION, Windmill Avenue, Kettering, Northamptonshire. 01536 410252.

TRURO COLLEGE, College Road, Truro, Cornwall TR1 3XX. 01872 264251.

UNIVERSITY COLLEGE NORTHAMPTON, Park Campus, Broughton Green Road, Northampton, NN2 7AL www.northampton.ac.uk 01604 735500

UNIVERSITY OF GLAMORGAN, School of Humanities and Social Sciences, Pontypridd, Mid Glamorgan CF37 1DL www.glam.ac.uk 01433 480480

UNIVERSITY OF KINGSTON, School of Music, Kingston Hill, Kingston-Upon-Thames, Surrey KT2 7LB. www.kingston.ac.uk 020 8547 7149

UNIVERSITY OF LINCOLNSHIRE AND HUMBERSIDE, Hull School of Art and Design, Queens Gardens, Hull HU1 3DQ www.ulh.ac.uk 01482 440550

UNIVERSITY OF SALFORD, Salford M5 4WT www.salford.ac.uk 0161 295 5321

UNIVERSITY OF SUSSEX, Media Studies Faculty, Essex House, Brighton BN1 9RQ www.sussex.ac.uk 01273 678019

UNIVERSITY OF TEESIDE, School of Law, Arts and Humanities, Middlesborough, Cleveland, TS1 3BA www.tees.ac.uk 01642 384019

UNIVERSITY OF WALES NEWPORT, Caerleon Campus PO Box 179 Newport NP18 1YG www.newport.ac.uk 01633 430088

UNIVERSITY OF WOLVERHAMPTON, Wolverhampton Science Park, Wolverhampton WV10 9RY www.wlv.ac.uk 01902 824003

UXBRIDGE COLLEGE, Park Road, Uxbridge, Middlesex, UB8 1NQ. www.uxbridge.ac.uk 01895 853510.

VARNDEAN COLLEGE, Surrenden Road, Brighton, East Sussex, BN1 6WQ. www.varndean.ac.uk 01273 508011.
WAKEFIELD COLLEGE, Thornes Park Centre, Thornes Park, Wakefield, WF2 2QZ. www.wakcoll.ac.uk 01924 789808.

WALSAL COLEGE OF ARTS AND TECHNOLOGY, Shelley Centre, Scarborough Road, Pleck, Walsall WS2 2TY. 01922 720889.

WARWICKSHIRE COLLEGE, Warwick New Road, Leamington Spa, Warwickshire, CV32 5JE. www.warkscol.ac.uk 01926 318000.

WEST HERTS COLLEGE, School of Business and Management, Hempstead Road, Watford WD17 3EZ. www.westherts.ac.uk 01923 812592.

WEST NOTTINGHAMSHIRE COLLEGE, Derby Road, Mansfield, Notts, NG18 5BH. www.westnotts.ac.uk 01623 627191.

WEST THAMES COLLEGE, London Road, Isleworth, Middlesex TW7 4HS. 020 8568 2331.

WESTMINSTER ADULT EDUCATION SERVICE, Ebury Bridge Centre, 4 Sutherland Street, London SW1 4LH. www.waes.ac.uk 020 7641 7852.

WESTMINSTER KINGSWAY COLLEGE, Battersea Park Road, London SW11 4JR. www.wesking.ac.uk 020 7556 8000.

WIGAN AND LEIGH COLLEGE, The Media Centre, leigh Campus, Railway Road, Leigh WN7 4AH. www.wigan-leigh.ac.uk 01942 761729.

WILTSHIRE COLLEGE CHIPPENHAM, Cocklebury Road, Chippenham, Wiltshire, SN15 3QD. www.wiltscoll.ac.uk. 01249 464444.

WIMBLEDON SCHOOL OF ART, Merton Hall Road, London SW19 3QA www.wwwcbguides.com 020 8408 5080

WOLVERHAMPTON COLLEGE, Wulfrun Campus, Paget Road, Wolverhampton WV6 ODU. www.wolverhamptoncollege.ac.uk 01902 317700.

WYKE COLLEGE, Grammar School Road, Hull HU5 4NX. www.hull.ac.uk/hull/ctls-web/wyke.html 01978 311794.

YMTC (YORKSHIRE MEDIA TRAINING CONSORTIUM) 40 Hanover Square, Leeds, LS3 1BQ. (New Entrants) www.ymtc.co.uk 0113 294 4410.

YORK COLLEGE, Tadcaster Road, York YO24 1UA. www.yorkcollege.ac.uk. 01904 770294.

SHORT COURSES
There are over 170 centres in England Scotland, Wales and Northern Ireland offering short courses. These courses range from one-day events through to part time evening

classes and to courses lasting for several weeks. The centres include colleges of further education and higher education, film and video workshops and commercial training centres.

For course titles, duration, entry requirements and cost, see media and multimedia short courses, which is produced jointly by the British Film Institute and Skillset. This is available from Plymbridge Distributors Ltd, Estover Road, Plymouth, Devon PL6 7PZ. Tel: 01752 202301. Priced currently at £4.50.

The short courses information may also be found on the British Film Institute website www.bfi.org.uk/mediacourses.

ABERDEEN COLLEGE, Gallowgate, Aberdeen, Scotland AB25 1BN. www.abcol.ac.uk 01224 612325.

ACADEMY OF RADIO,FILM AND TELEVISION, American Building, 79A Tottenham Court Road, London W1T 4TD. www.londonacademy.co.uk 020 84048298.

AMERSHAM AND WYCOMBE COLLEGE, Stanley Hil, Amersham, Bucks HP7 9HN. www.amersham.ac.uk 01494 735555.

THE ARIEL TRUST LTD, Floor 3, Graphic House, Duke Street, Liverpool, L1 4JR.www.arieltrust.com 0151708 0595.
ARISTA, 11 Wells Mews, London W1P 3FL. 020 7323 1775.

THE ARVON FOUNDATION, Lumb Bank, Heptonstall, Hebden Bridge, West Yorkshire HX7 6DF. www.arvonfoundation.org 01422 843714.

AVRIL ROWLANDS TV TRAINING FOR PRODUCTION ASSISTANTS, Laxford House, Poplar piece, Inkberrow, Worcs WR7 4JD. www.avriltrain.com 01368 792051.

BBC TRAINING AND DEVELOPMENT, BBC New Media Training, 35 Marylebone High Street, London W1U 4PX. www.bbctraining.co.uk 020 7208 9426.

BBC TRAINING AND DEVELOPMENT, Wood Norton, Evesham, Worcs WR11 4YB. www.bbctraining.co.uk 0870 122 0216.

BEXLEY COLLEGE, St Josephs Campus, 269 Woolwich Road, Abbeywood, London SE2 OAR. www.bexley.ac.uk 01322 404277.

BIRKBECK COLLEGE, Faculty of Continuing Education (Media Studies), 26 Russell Street, London WC1B 5DQ. www.bbk.ac.uk 020 7631 6667.

BKSTS – THE MOVING IMAGE SOCIETY, 5 walpole Court, Ealing Studios, Ealing Green, London W5 5ED. www.bksts.com 020 8584 5220

BLACKBURN COLLEGE, The Media Centre, Fielden Street, Blackburn, Lancashire BB2 1LH. 01254 682700.

BLAKE COLLEGE, 167 New Cavendish Street, London W1M 7FJ. www.blake.ac.uk 020 7636 0658.

BLAZE THE TRAIL LTD, 2nd Floor, 241 High Street, Walthamstow, London E17 7BH. www.blaze-the-trail.com 020 8520 4569.

BRADFORD COMMUNITY BROADCASTING, 2 Forster Square Bradford BD1 1DQ. www.bcb.yorks.com 01274 771677.

BRIGHTON COLLEGE OF TECHNOLOGY, Pelham Street, Brighton, BN1 4FA. www.bricoltech.ac.uk 01273 66738.

BRITISH UNIVERSITIES FILM AND VIDEO COUNCIL, 77 Wells Street, London W1T 3QJ. www.bvfc.ac.uk 020 7393 1504.

CAMBERWELL COLLEGE OF ARTS, Developments at London Institute (DALI), Peckham Road, London SE5 8UF. www.camb.linst.ac.uk. 020 7514 6311.

INIVERSITY OF CAMBRIDGE, Board of Continuing Education, Madingley Hall, Madingley, Cambridge CB3 8AQ. www.cont-ed.cam.ac.uk 01954 280226.

CENTRAL SAINT MARTINS COLLEGE OF ART AND DESIGN, Short Course Office, Southampton Row,London WC1B 4AP. www.csm.linst.ac.uk/shortcourse 020 7514 7015.

CHELSEA COLLEGE OF ART AND DESIGN, Developments at London Institute (DALI), Hugon Road, London SW6 3ES. www.chelsea.linst.ac.uk 020 7514 6311.

THE CHILDRENS FILM UNIT, South Way, Leavesden, Herts WD2 7LZ. www.btinternet.com/-cfu 01923 354656.

THE CINEMA AND FILM WORKSHOP DEPT, Chapter Arts Centre, Market Road, Canton,Cardiff CF5 1QE. 029 2031 1050.

CLINTEL INTERNATIONAL, Watton Road, Ware, Herts SG12 OAE. www.cintel.co.uk 01920 463939.
CIRENCESTER COLLEGE, Stroud Road, Cirencester, Glos GL7 1XA. 01285 640994.

CITY AND ISLINGTON COLLEGE, Islington Campus, 444 Camden Road, London N7 OSP. www.candi.ac.uk 020 7700 8600.

CITY COLLEGE BRIGHTON AND HOVE, Pelham Street, Brighton, BN1 4FA. www.cch.ac.uk. 01273 667738.

CITY EYE LTD, 1st Floor, Northam Centre, Kent Street, Northam, Southampton SO14 5SP. www.city-eye.co.uk. 023 8063 4177.

THE CITY LITERARY INSTITUTE, Stukeley Street, London WC2B 5LJ. 020 7430 0542.

CITY OF BRISTOL COLLEGE, Ashley Down Road, Ashley Down, Bristol BS7 9BU. www.cityofbristol.ac.uk. 0117 904 5143.

CITY UNIVERSITY, Courses for Adults, Northampton Square, London EC1V OHB. www.city.ac.uk/contel.cfa.htm 020 7040 8268.

CLOCKTOWER MEDIA TRAINING, Croydon Clocktower, Katherine Street, Croydon CR9 1ET. www.croydon.gov.uk/media 020 8760 5400.

COMMUNITY MEDIA ASSOCIATION, 15 Paternoster Place, Sheffiled S1 2BX. www.commedia.org.uk 0114 279 5219.

CONNECTIONS COMMUNICATIONS CENTRE, Palingwick House, 241 King Street, Hammersmith, London W6 9LP. www.cccmedia.co.uk 020 8741 1766.

CORNWALL MEDIA RESOURCE, Royal Circus Buildings, Back Lane west, Redruth, Cornwall TR15 2BT. www.mediasource.freeserve.co.uk 01209 218288.

CRICKLADE COLLEGE, Charlton Road, Andover, Hampshire SP10 1EJ. www.cricklade.ac.uk 01264 334222.

CSV DUNDEE MEDIA ACTION, Unit H, Market Mews, Broughty Ferry Road, Dundee DD1 3NH. 01382 451840.

CSV MEDIA MIDLANDS, Hollymoor Multimedia centre, Manor Park Grove, Off Tessall Lane, Northfield, Birmingham B31 5ER. 0121 683 1800.

DELAMAR ACADEMY OF MAKE-UP, 52A Waltham Grove, Fulham, London SW6 1QR. www.themake-upcentre.co.uk 020 7381 0213.

DERRY MEDIA ACCESS AND LOCAL TV NETWORK, Foyles Arts Centre, Lawrence Hill, Derry, Londonderry BT48 7NJ. 028 7137 0091.

EALING THE COLLEGE, Ealing Centre, The Green, Ealing, London W5 5EW. www.etc.ac.uk 020 8231 6006.

EAST SURREY COLLEGE, Media Division, Gaton Point North, Claremont Road, Redhill, Surrey RH1 2JX. www.esc.org.uk 01737 772611.

UNIVERSITY OF EDINBURGH, Centre for Continuing Education, 11 Buccleuch Place, Edinburgh EH8 9LW. www.cce.ed.ac.uk 0131 650 3073.

EUROSCRIPT, Screenwriters Centre Suffolk house, 1-8 Whitfield Place, London W1T 5JU www.euroscript.co.uk 020 7387 5880.

Fareham College, Bishopsfield Road, Fareham, Hampshire, PO14 1NH. www.fareham.ac.uk. 01329 815200.

FILM NAND VIDEO ACCESS CENTRE, 25A SW Thistle street lane, Edinburgh EH1 22EW. www.fva-online.com 0131 220 0220.

FOUR CORNERS FILM WORKSHOP, 113 Roman Road, Bethnal Green, London E2 OQN. www.fourcornersfilm.org.uk 020 8981 4243.

GATESHEAD COLLEGE, Durham Road, Gateshead, Tyne and wear NE9 5BN. 0191 490 2474.

GLASGOW MEDIA ACCESS CENTRE, 3rd Floor, 34 Albion Street, Glasgow G1 1LH. www.g-mac.co.uk 0141 553 2620.

HACKNEY COMMUNITY COLLEGE, Shoreditch Campus, Falkirk Street, London N1 6HQ. www.comm-coll-hackney.ac.uk 020 7613 9123.

HAMMERSMITH AND WEST LONDON COLLEGE, Gliddon Road, Barons Court, London W14 9BL. www.hwlc.ac.uk. 020 8741 1688.

HARLOW COLLEGE, Velizy Avenue, Harlow, Essex, CM20 3LH. www.harlow-college.ac.uk 01279 868000.

HOXTON HALL, 130 Hoxton Street, London N1 6SH. www.hoxtonhall.dabsol.co.uk 020 7684 0060.

HUDDERSFIELD TECHNICAL COLLEGE, New North Road, Huddersfield, HD1 5NN. 01484 348100.

HULL TIME BASED ARTS, 42-43 High Street, Hull HU1 1PS. www.timebase.org 01482 216446.

HULME ADULT LEARNING CENTRE, Hulme Walk, Hulme, Manchester M15 5FQ. 0161226 8441.

INTERMEDIA FILM AND VIDEO (NOTTINGHAM) LTD, 19 Heathcote Street, Nottingham, NG1 3AF. www.intermedianotts.co.uk 0115 95 6909.

INTERNATIONAL FILM SCHOOL WALES, University of Wales College, Newport, Caerleon Campus, PO Box 179, Newport NP18 3YG. www.ifsw.newport.ac.uk 01633 432679.

INVERNESS COLLEGE, 3 Longman Road, Longman South, Inverness, IV1 1SA. 01463 273353.

KENSINGTON AND CHELSEA COLLEGE, Hortensia Centre, Hortensia Road, London SW10 OQS. 020 7573 5346.

KILMARNOCK COLLEGE OF FURTHER EDUCATION, Holehouse Road, Kilmarnock, Ayrshire KA3 7AT. www.kilmarnock.ac.uk 01563 523501.

LAMBETH COLLEGE, Vauxhall Centre, Belmore Street, Wandsworth Road, London SW8 2JY. www.lambethcollege.ac.uk 020 7501 5259.

LEEDS ANIMATION WORKSHOP, 45 Bayswater Row, Leeds, West Yorkshire, LS8 5LF. 0113 248 4997.

LEEDS UNIVERSITY, School of Continuing Education, Leeds LS2 9JT. www.leeds.ac.uk/aed/cchome/sce.htm 0113 23 3205.

LIGHTHOUSE, 9-12 Middle Street, Brighton, BN1 1AL. www.lighthouse.org.uk 01273 384258.

LIGHTHOUSE, The Chubb Building, Fryer Street, Wolverhampton WV1 1HT. www.light-house.co.uk 01902 71605.

LONDON FILM ACADEMY, The Old Church, 52a Waltham Grove, London SW6 1QR. www.londonfilmacademy.com 020 7386 7711.

MEDIA PRODUCTION TRAINING FACILITIES, 1st Floor, 383 Brixton Road, London SW9 8BE. www.media-production.demon.co.uk 020 7737 7152.

METRO NEW MEDIA, 35 Kingsland Road, Shoreditch, London E2 8AA. www.metronewmedia.com 020 7729 9992.

MORLEY COLLEGE, 61 Westminster Bridge Road, London SE1 7HT. www.morleycollege.ac.uk. 020 7450 9235.

MOVING VISION, Wyvern Road, Newbridge on Wye, Powys, LD1 6LH. www.movingvision.co.uk. 01597 860575.

NATIONAL SHORT COURSE TRAINING PROGRAMME, National Film and Television School, Beaconsfield Studios, Station Road, Beaconsfield, Bucks HP9 1LG. www.nsftsfilm-tv.ac.uk 01494 677903.

NETWORK, 3 Harriers View, Banbury, Oxon, OX16 9JP. 01295 263273.

NEWCASTLE COLLEGE, Rye Hill Campus, Scotswood Road, Newcastle Upon Tyne NE4 7SA. www.ncl-coll.ac.uk 0191 200 4000.

UNIVERSITY OF NEWCASTLE UPON TYNE, Centre for Lifelong Learning, King George V1 Building, Queen Victoria Road, Newcastle Upon Tyne NE1 7RU. www.ncl.ac.uk 0191 222 6542.

NORTH BIRMINGHAM COLLEGE, Aldridge Road, Great Barr, Birmingham, B44 8NE. www.northbham.ac.uk 0121 325 2245.

NORTH EAST WORCESTERSHIRE COLLEGE, Redditch Campus, Peakman Street, Redditch, Worcs B98 8DW. 01527 570020.

NORTH KENSINGTON VIDEO DRAMA PROJECT, 1 Thorpe Close, London W10 5XL. 020 8964 2641.

NORTHERN FILM SCHOOL, Leeds Metropolitan University, 2 Queen Square, Leeds, LS2 8AF. www.lmu.ac.uk/hen/aad/nfs 0113 283 1900.

NORTHERN VISION MEDIA CENTRE, 4 Lower Donegall Street, Belfast BT1 2FN. www.northernvisions.org 028 9024 5495.

OXFORD FILM AND VIDEO MAKERS, The Stables, North Place, Headington, Oxford OX3 9HY. www.ofvm.org 01865 760074.

PAVILION, 2 Woodhouse Street, Leeds, LS3 1AD. www.pavilion.org.uk 0113 243 1749.

PERFORMING ARTS LABS, The Gym, Mary ward House, 5 Tavistock Place, London WC1H 9SN. 020 7387 96.

PERSONAL PRESENTATION LIMITED, Canalot Production Studios, 222 Kensal Road, London W10 5BN. www.personalpresentation.com 020 8968 0421.

PICTURE THIS MOVING IMAGE, Spike Island Studios, 40 Sydney Row, Bristol BS1 6UU. 0117 925 7010.

POZITIV PRODUCTIONS, PO Box 2646, Burghfield Mill, Reading, Berkshire, RG30 3YH. www.pozitiv.com 0118950 9050.

PRESENTER-LED PRODUCTIONS, PO BOX 17861, London W5 5ZP. www.presenterled.com 07074 737597.

RAVENSBOURNE COLLEGE OF DESIGN AND COMMUNICATION, Short Course Unit, Walden Road, Chislehurst, Kent BR7 5SN. www.rave.ac.uk/shortcourses 020 8325 8323.

REAL TIME, The Media Centre, 21 South Street Arts Centre, Reading, RG1 4QU. www.rael-time.org.uk 0118 901 5205.

SAFESETS TRAINING, Stable Studios, 15 Priest End, Thame, Oxon, OX9 2AE. www.productiondesign.co.uk 01844218072

THE SCREENWRITERS WORKSHOP, Suffolk House, 1-8 Whitfield Place, London W1T 5JU. www.lsw.org.uk 020 7387 5511.

SCRENE PRODUCTIONS, 126 Norwood Road, London SE24 9AF. www.screne.org 020 8671 7071.

SIF (SHEFFIELD INDEPENDENT FILM) 5 Brown Street, Sheffield, S1 2BS. 0114 272 0304.

UNIVERSITY OF SUSSEX, Centre for Continuing Education, Falmer, Brighton, BN1 9RG. www.sussex.ac.uk. 01273 606755

THAMES VALLEY UNIVERSITY, St Mary's Road, Ealing, London W5 5RF. www.tvu.ac.uk 020 8579 5000

TRANSITION MEDIA ARTS, Wellington House, 83 Main Road, Washingborough, Lincoln, LN4 1AY.
Beehive.thisislincolnshire.co.uk/transitionmedia 01522 797207.

VFG LIGHTING, Pinewood Studios, Iver Heath, Buckinghamshire, SLO ONH. 020 8795 7000.

WARPAINT SCHOOL OF MAKEUP, 7 Hadleigh Close, Merton Park, London SW20 9AW. 020 8543 1996.

WEST HERTS MEDIA TRAINING CENTRE, South Way, Leavesden Herts WD2 7LZ. 01923 681602.

UNIVERSITY OF THE WEST OF ENGLAND BRISTOL, Media Works, Faculty of Art Media and Design, Kennel Lodge Road, Bower Ashton, Bristol, BS1 2JT. www.mediaworks.org.uk 0117 927 5881

WESTMINSTER KINGSWAY COLLEGE, Battersea park Road, London SW11 4JR. www.wesking.ac.uk. 020 7556 8000.

WFA MEDIA AND CULTURAL CENTRE, 9 Lucy Street, Manchester, M15 4BX. www.wfamedia.co.uk 0161 848 9785.

WOMENS INDEPENDENT CINEMA HOUSE, 40 Rodney Street, Liverpool, L1 9AA. 0151 707 0539.

YMTC (Yorkshire Media Training Consortium), 40 Hanover Square, leeds, LS3 1BQ. www.ymtc.co.uk 0113 294 4410.

YORK MULTIMEDIA NETWORK, Gateway House, 26 Swinegate, York, YO1 8AZ. www.ymn.net

Other courses

In addition to the above colleges offering courses in further education and short courses, there are a range of undergradute and postgraduate courses on offer. These courses can be the BFI Media Courses UK, as listed, or through the BFI website.

Appendix 1 Sources of funding for filmmaking

Funding for short and low-budget films
There is money around, quite substantial sums in fact, to support filmmakers at the start of their careers. The 'Low Budget Funding Guide' published by the British Film Institute lists sources of such funds, which are usually given in the form of loans which have to be repaid only if the film goes into profit.

Most young filmmakers will get advice about local initiatives and funding possibilities through their Regional Art Boards. In London, responsibility is divided between the London Film and Video Development Agency and the London Production Fund. Other sources include:

- The broadcasters
- BFI New Directors Scheme
- British Screen Finance (now part of the Film Council)
- British Council (help with festivals etc)
- Local initiatives e.g. the Glasgow Film Fund
- Local Authority Arts Departments

There are also European and Pan European sources of funding – especially for co-productions and films which will offer work and training in areas requiring urban regeneration.

Applying for public funding
There are a few important rules to abide by when it comes to applying for any sort of public funding to make a film. As only a few applications are successful, these rules should be observed. They are:

- Potential backers will look for some sort of track record of 'delivering the goods'. Make sure that you can supply this evidence.
- When making an application, be professional
- Read the notes to the application and follow the instructions. Many people ignore this crucial aspect. You have to demonstrate that the work is achievable within time and budget.

- Team applications work best, when an individuals strengths and weaknesses are balanced by others.
- Find out what drives and interests different funders. For example Lottery applications like to hear about creativity and audience appeal, the European Regional Development Fund needs information about the economic sustainability of your project and the contribution it will make to your region.
- The chance of raising money for a film correlates with how well and concisely you can tell the story.

Before you apply for any funding get advice and understand the level of competition. Earlier funding is often easier to access in areas outside London, as there is less demand.

Getting development money

As we saw in chapter 2, The Film Policy Review Group identified the relative lack of emphasis on development within the British film industry. Traditionally, it has been very hard to get any financial support at this stage. A development budget may include:

- Office overheads
- Expenses (travel, etc)
- Research
- Pilot costs
- Fees for scriptwriters

To increase your own chances of funding it is very wise to concentrate on this last critical area. As we saw, the Film Council has identified that script writing and script editing as a skills shortage. Writers and editors are being encouraged to collaborate with others to provide high quality scripts. In the future it is probable that applications for funding may be based on a successful development stage.

146

Grants from public funds

The Department for Culture, Media and Sport has introduced a range of new initiatives with the intention of supporting and developing film culture and education. As we saw in chapter 2, the Film Council was created in 2000 to influence strategy for government support and industry liaison across the film production, exhibition and distribution agencies. As a result of this creation of a single agency to handle public finances and other initiatives, regional funding arrangements are also in a state of evolution. Scotland, Wales and Northern Ireland all have dedicated funds to support local creative talent, which will be distributed through the relevant national organisations – Scottish Screen, Sgrin and the Northern Ireland Film Commission.

NESTA – National Endowment for science, Technology and the Arts - is another government initiative which aims to encourage talented individuals and companies. It will be particularly interested in helping to turn ideas into 'bankable employment generating businesses which may be of particular interest to young production companies.

NESTA
33 Throgmorton Street, London EC2N 2BR.

Finding out about funding

The British Film Institute publishes an invaluable booklet, *Lowdown* – a low-budget funding guide, which provides invaluable relevant information on funding and the different bodies offering funding.

INDEX

155